LEGEND OF THE HOLY GRAIL

THE ORIGIN

OF THE

LEGEND OF THE HOLY GRAIL

WITH AN ACCOUNT OF SOME OTHER MEDIÆVAL
LEGENDS AND TRADITIONS.

BY

CHARLES MacDOUALL, LL.D.,
Late Professor of Greek in Queen's College, Belfast.

Books Ulster

First published in 1903 by Williams & Norgate, London, and William Mullan, Belfast.

This new edition, with reset text, published in 2015.

Typographical arrangement © Books Ulster.

ISBN 978-1-910375-31-0 (Paperback)

All rights reserved. No part of this publication may be reproduced, stored in a retrieval system, or transmitted by any means, electronic, mechanical, photocopying or otherwise, without the prior permission of the publisher.

The cover features the painting *The Siege and Destruction of Jerusalem by the Romans under the Command of Titus, A.D. 70*, (1850) by David Roberts.

PUBLISHER'S NOTE

The Origin of the Legend of the Holy Grail was first published in 1903, twenty years after the death of its author, Charles MacDouall, who was first Professor of Latin and second Professor of Greek at Queen's College (now Queen' University), Belfast. The editing of the manuscript was undertaken by his friend and former college librarian, Albert Ludwig Meissner (1832-1909). This new edition has had the text reset and several obvious typographical errors corrected although, despite due care, it is perfectly conceivable that fresh ones have been created, but these should be relatively few and far between. There was some inconsistency in the italicising of referenced book titles and also in the use of accents in the 1903 edition—for example, the name 'du Meril' was sometimes spelt with an acute accent over the 'e', once with a grave, but usually with no accent at all. These inconsistencies have generally been left as they were.

PREFACE

EVER since the publication of Niebuhr's Roman History the study of ancient traditions and legends, of popular beliefs and customs has attracted the attention of inquirers. A new critical school of historians arose who questioned every fact and tradition. Facts, hitherto undoubted, were relegated to the realm of fable, whilst undoubted myths were shown to be the expression of general truths and not mere isolated historical incidents; an observation made long ago by Aristotle. Soon this critical method was applied to the history of religious beliefs. Jacob Grimm, in his *Deutsche Mythologie*, showed the gradual transformation of the old heathen gods, the gods that were no more, into demons and sprites, under the influence of Christianity. The study of mediaeval history and literature, the publication of books and documents hitherto accessible only to the few, and even that under great difficulties, let in a flood of light on, what had been up to then in very truth, the dark ages. Before this, the rise and growth of the imperial and papal powers, their struggles and rivalries, had been thought the principal, if not the only subject of interest to the historian of the Middle Ages. The great store of religious traditions, the legends of Saints and Martyrs, were looked upon as the inventions of knavish monks and priests. Deliberate invention, and even fraud, no doubt, there has been. But nothing, on the other hand, gives us so deep an insight into the life and thought of the people as just these legends. The foremost place amongst these legends is held by the story of King Arthur and the Knights of the Table Round, which, after inspiring the greatest poets of mediæval Europe, has proved a never-failing source of poetic inspiration to the poets of Modern Europe.

PREFACE

To trace the origin and gradual rise of these traditions has been the object of many scholars especially in France and Germany. Though much has been done, much more remains to be done. It had been the aim of the late Dr. MacDouall to write a complete account of the origin and development of the Legend of the Holy Grail, giving not only the results of the researches of others, but of his own wide and varied reading and cautious critical judgment. Death prevented him from carrying out this design, and, what is here offered, is only an introduction which he dictated, after having lost his sight, to the companion of his life and labours. Those who have but a superficial knowledge of Mediæval Literature have no idea of the amount of labour demanded by such an undertaking. The pages here presented to the reader will give an insight into the manifold and intricate ramifications of the subject. Many a fact, seemingly insignificant, many a statement, on the very face of it absurd, assume a different complexion and a deeper meaning, when brought into line with other facts and other statements, taken singly, equally insignificant and equally absurd.

To me, whose studies, to a great extent, have been mediæval, the reading of these pages has been a renewal of the many pleasant hours passed in instructive conversation with my late friend. On no occasion did I leave him without being the better and the wiser. His marvellous memory often enabled him, when he was totally blind, to direct me, not only to a particular volume, but to the particular part of it, the right or the left-hand page, the top or the bottom.

To others, his friends, and among them, especially to his former pupils, these pages will bring back the living form of the revered teacher, with all his learning, his zeal and his modesty. Those who attended his lectures in Queen's College, Belfast, had the good fortune of being trained by a band of

PREFACE

distinguished and enthusiastic teachers: Thomas Andrews, Peter Tait, George L. Craik, Charles Reichel, James M'Cosh, George Dickie, Wyville Thomson. It was indeed the golden age of the Queen's College, the memory of which casts forward even now a ray of sunlight.

But to no one have these pages the same interest as to her, the faithful companion of his life and labours, who from his lips took down the words of this book which now she modestly offers "to his old friends and pupils to whom it may be welcome for his sake, even if the subject should be in itself of little interest to them."

And we, receiving this gift thankfully, answer this greeting of our friend and master from beyond the grave with a reverent and loving farewell.

HAVE PIA ANIMA!

A. L. MEISSNER.

CONTENTS

PAGE

CHAPTER I.
THE LEGEND OF THE SANGREAL — 1

CHAPTER II.
APOCRYPHAL AND EARLY LEGENDS ABOUT JOSEPH OF ARIMATHÆA AND NICODEMUS — 8

CHAPTER III.
LATER LEGENDS EMBODIED IN LATIN DOCUMENTS — 16

CHAPTER IV.
SECTION I.—DISCREPANCIES IN THE LATIN LEGENDS CONCERNING PILATE — 20

SECTION II.—THE FATE OF PILATE AND THE DESTRUCTION OF JERUSALEM ASSOCIATED IN AQUITANIAN LEGENDS — 24

CHAPTER V.
JOSEPH AND NICODEMUS IN JUDEA — 31

CHAPTER VI.
MIGRATIONS FROM PALESTINE TO WESTERN EUROPE IN THE APOSTOLIC AGE — 42

CONTENTS

	PAGE
SECTION I.—LEGENDS ABOUT THE APOSTLES JAMES AND PHILIP IN SPAIN AND GAUL	44
SECTION II.—LEGENDS ABOUT DIONYSIUS AMONG THE FRANKS, AND THE BETHANIAN FAMILY AMONG THE PROVENÇALS	54

CHAPTER VII.

GLASTONBURY AND ITS TRADITIONS OF JOSEPH OF ARIMATHÆA, OF ST. PATRICK, AND OF OTHER SAINTLY VISITORS ... 69

CHAPTER VIII.

GLASTONBURY, THE BURIAL PLACE OF SAINTS AND HEROES ... 95

APPENDIX TO CHAPTER IV.

THE EARLIER HISTORY OF PILATE ... 107

APPENDIX TO CHAPTER VI., SECTION II.

SEQUEL OF THE PROVENÇAL LEGEND ... 111

NOTES ... 125

CHAPTER I.

The Legend of the Sangreal

IT is generally admitted that the interest felt in Hagiology—in the legendary lore of sacred reliques, as well as that of martyrs, confessors, and thaumaturgic saints—is greatly enhanced to intelligent devotees, and is often mainly constituted in the view of dispassionate students, by elements of quite an accessory character. Sceptical historians, as frankly as others, confess their obligations to the guidance of Hagiology for revelations respecting periods and events where more pretentious authorities are at fault,—for gleams of light reflected upon institutions, habits, and states of society otherwise unintelligible,—for elucidation both of oral traditions and of literary monuments arbitrarily associated with them,—of traditions rooted in heathenism,—and of literary works of a secular cast not easily reconcilable to Christian ideas, or even more or less antagonistic to them.

But the work of extricating what is essential from what is adventitious, so as to ascertain the true character, the origin, the development, and the scope of either the one portion or the other, is found to be proportionately difficult. So multifarious are the accretions, so ambiguous in their import, so incongruous with the central matter, and so ill-adjusted to each other that even critical tact shrinks from pronouncing upon the tone of the complex whole, or upon the functions of the several elements which are combined in it. Thus we find the pilgrimages and adventures of early Christian Missionaries

THE HOLY GRAIL

most perplexingly worked up in the tissue of princely pedigrees or in the blazonry of knightly orders, at once military and monastic, whose rules boasted the sanction of apostolic antiquity, or in the annals of confraternities, cities, and nations which looked up to saints of the earliest centuries as their Tutelars; and thus, not only in secular chronicles or in didactic and lyrical compositions, but also throughout elaborate romances dedicated to profane chivalry, and to love, not always hallowed, we find such incongruous personages intervening as St. James, St. Andrew, St. David, and other champions of Christendom.

So, too, in regard to holy reliques, whether such as admitted of being amicably disparted for the benefit of widely scattered communities, or such, as, being in the natural course of things one and indivisible, were yet exhibited entire at the same time in numerous shrines, giving origin to unedifying feuds among the claimants of the honors, immunities, and emoluments which were implied or secured in their possession.

The accounts current in various localities about the transmission from the earliest periods of these palladia, as if they had not been in themselves sufficiently trying even to robust faith, were in course of time completely immeshed in a web of unconnected legends which grew up about rival monasteries, cathedrals and municipalities. Instances in profusion will occur to the memory, even if we exclude from view all but the memorials of the Last Supper, the life, the passion and burial of our Lord Himself. Such for example were the seamless tunic, which has been enshrined for centuries back, entire or in portions, in Trèves and some twenty-five places besides, the crown of thorns, the purple robe, the sponge, the spear which drew forth the sacred blood and the charger which caught it as it flowed. Such again as the table, the carving knife, and the chalice which were used at the institution of the Eucharist.

MEDIÆVAL LEGENDS

Several of the articles last mentioned are closely associated with each other in the Legend of the Saint Graal. Moreover, the principal personages in that Legend are represented as having been commissioned and instructed by the Saviour Himself. It was occupied primarily with Joseph of Arimathea* (the noble Decurion) who, through the favour of Pilate the Roman Governor, and with the co-operation of Nicodemus (a member of the Sanhedrim), interred the sacred body, performing the last offices himself, and with the graces and virtues of a marvellous vessel, in which Joseph was said to have preserved the blood from the crucifixion wounds—a vessel which had also a prior claim to veneration as having been used at the last supper.

The compilers of the story rehearsed the various fates and fortunes of the Arimathean family, and of such kinsfolk and countrymen as were associated with them, first on their native soil, afterwards in their migrations overland into Mesopotamia and by sea to the distant West, as far, perhaps, as the British Islands; and being quite untrammeled by any conceptions of congruity, whether historic or chronological or geographical, they availed themselves of travellers' tales and seamen's yarns in constructing episodes that teemed with wild and wonderful material.

Among the ecclesiastical legends of the Middle Ages this one has had an exceptional good fortune, inasmuch as it acquired an extensive popularity among classes which its influence could hardly have been expected to reach while it retained its original form; and it has continued down to

---

* Parole já sainte escripture del Graal d'un gentil cevalier ki estoit á cel tems, qui avoit à non Joseph d'Arimachie.—Et moult était piteus et dous et de grand relegyon et si avoit reçue la créance Jhésu Crist."—Le Saint Graal, ed. E. Hucher, t. ll. pp. 47, 48.

THE HOLY GRAIL

the present day to be potential in moulding and enriching the imaginative literature of Western Europe, amid manifold revolutions in thought and taste and sentiment. Such results have followed since the brilliant Trouvères of the 12th and 13th centuries took up the narrative, already so far developed, and saw fit to interweave it with their tales of chivalry, especially with those which concerned the Court and the Table Round of Arthur,—"begirt with British and Armoric knights,"—some of whom were represented as of Arimathean lineage, and as thereby especially privileged to engage in a quest for the mystic vessel which they regarded as an heirloom. For the religious element, no longer circumscribed in its operation within the records of cloister-life, of mission work, of martyrdoms, and wholesale conversions, but viewed as the mainspring of secular enterprise in all the various phases which courtly poets and romancers cared to depict, as on the one hand it elevated the tone and chastened the spirit of the compositions into which it was now infused, so on the other hand it acquired for its own primitive and quaint embodiments a share in that charmed life which is still enjoyed by epic romances of the Arthurian cycle.

In course of time the legend was still further transfigured by poets who, accustomed to unlimited license in varying fictions of a secular type, showed themselves as little embarrassed by scruples about preserving unimpaired the texture of the church legends which they had begun to handle. Exercising their inventive faculties, some of them proceeded to substitute for what appeared to them too simple an origin for the wondrous vessel one of a more transcendental character. Passing in silence its Arimathean guardian, and obscuring even its Arthurian associations, they assigned its custody to a dynasty which had its origin not in Palestine but in Upper Asia, and its royal seat not in Britain but on the Continent.

MEDIÆVAL LEGENDS

The innovations in this sense hazarded by Chretien de Troye were indeed negative and unobtrusive, while those which Wolfram von Eschenbach subsequently presented were very pronounced and sensational. But neither the milder nor the bolder novelties appear to have found favour with contemporaries, and the continuators of both the French and the German poem suggested expedients for reconciling their tenor with the previously accepted tradition, from which they wished it to appear that there had been no intentional deflection. It is the Arimathean and Arthurian phasis of the legend that has attracted the sympathies of such interpreters as Spencer, Milton, and Tennyson; and it is clearly with it that any critical investigation should deal in the outset, both because it is the simplest and the most primitive and because it is recognised in outline by the oldest authorities.

But even in its most primitive form, as a purely ecclesiastical legend, it is difficult to find a full and satisfactory explanation of its origin and to trace its history and development; and when it becomes connected with another set of Legends, the Romances that have gathered around the name of Arthur and when his Knights become involved in the mysteries of "The Holy Grail," the path through those forests of adventure becomes very bewildering to the investigator. Every precaution therefore will be needful in order to discriminate as far as possible the old and essential elements of the tradition from those which are of foreign origin, of more recent growth, and which are ornamental rather than significant. We must endeavour at every step to approximate the age, to circumscribe the locality and to test the credibility of the authorities relied on; and this, whether they be extrinsic to our subject and consulted only for elucidation of particular points, or primary as being the very sources from which are drawn the traditions which we shall have to review. Indeed in regard to

THE HOLY GRAIL

those primary documents we must be prepared to find that they claim a wildly exaggerated antiquity, and that their alleged parentage is very doubtful, if not wholly fictitious, even when they do not, as some of them do, advance pretensions to a supernatural origin.

The preceding considerations suggest the course to be pursued in the following pages.

We shall first succinctly report the early though extra-canonical notices regarding Joseph, with his friends and followers, which leave them still in their native country or on its borders, and then the later accounts of their journeyings and adventures in foreign climes, extending as far as the British Isles. It will be found that Nicodemus also acts a prominent part in the earlier transactions, but he afterwards falls into the background, and only on rare occasions comes into view.

Next we shall speak of the San Greal, indicating the nature of its connection with those saintly wanderers, the influence which it exercised upon their own fortunes and upon the objects of their mission, and the way in which it was covertly preserved somewhere in Britain during an indefinitely long period by their descendants.

Thirdly we shall advert to the efforts put forth to secure its tutelage for the Court of King Arthur, and the Quest undertaken by a number of his Knights,—one of whom succeeded in acquiring it, and carried it back into Asia.

Lastly we shall give an account of the experiments made by some poets, who treated the Greal, apart altogether from Arimathean or British associations, as a jewel fallen from Heaven, carefully guarded by a royal Hierarchy somewhere near the Pyrenees, and ultimately carried by its latest custodian into the realm of Prester John.

It is only after all the representations derived from documentary sources shall have been exhaustively treated, that

MEDIÆVAL LEGENDS

it will be allowable to pass into the province of speculation, and to review certain analogies which have been, or which may be, traced between the tradition of the Greal and myths or legends of other times and countries. We may, therefore, be ultimately called upon to consider, not only whether the Arimathean tradition may have been variously modified or supplemented from Keltic or Oriental fictions, but also whether the very core of it is really as original as it seems, or whether it was known under another form, before it was adapted to Christian symbolism and linked with a Christian confessor, having been borrowed from a pre-Christian system, of which it was a legitimate and undoubted outgrowth, and which presented many points in common with the hagiology and ritual of both Eastern and Western Churches.

CHAPTER II.

Apocryphal and Early Legends about Joseph of Arimathea and Nicodemus.

IN seeking for the earliest suggestion that might have led to the wonderful story told of Joseph of Arimathea, and the part assigned to him in the Legend of the Sangreal we find the germ of it, it may be, in an apocryphal account of the trial, the crucifixion, the burial and the resurrection of our Lord, which introduces Joseph and Nicodemus and Veronica, as well as Pilate, Caiaphas, and many other persons who are represented as taking part in the trial, and in the events that followed.*

This account is embodied in a Greek document, which appears to have been sketched about A.D. 361-3, and expanded to the shape in which it is extant early in the 5th century, probably about A.D. 425, and in a Latin translation of this which was made shortly after.† The title, admitting some variations, runs thus: Ὑπομνήματα τοῦ Κυρίου ἡμῶν Ἰησοῦ Χριστοῦ πραχθέντα ἐπὶ Ποντίου Πιλάτου "a record" (or "minutes") "of the Acts and Passion of our Lord under Pontius Pilate." In Latin it is sometimes entitled more briefly *Salvatoris Gesta* "Acts of the Saviour," or else less properly *Acta* or *Gesta Pilati*. The latter form, intended to represent "Transactions under Pilate," is the one cited by Gregory, Bishop of Tours, who, before A.D. 590, borrowed some particulars from these "Gesta Pilati" in his *Historia Francorum*. He refers particularly to the account of Joseph's imprisonment and his miraculous

---

* Notes, Note 1.

† Notes, Note 2.

MEDIÆVAL LEGENDS

release (cc. XXI. XXIV.)*

Of equal or superior antiquity is another work, narrating "Christ's Descent into Hades." This, we are told, was written during their brief sojourn on earth, by two of those who had risen from the dead with our Lord, Leucius and Charinus, sons of Simeon, and handed by them, before they returned to their graves, one copy to Joseph and Nicodemus, and one to Annas and Caiaphas. While this curious document is found in connection with the Gesta in hardly any of the Greek MSS., the Latin version, belonging probably to the 5th century, is, in most if not all copies of the Latin version of the Gesta, united with it, as if it were the latter part of the same narration; and the work so made up has been known since the time of Charlemagne under the title *Evangelium Nicodemi*, though occasionally bearing other titles, such as *Passio Christi*.†

The early, wide, and enduring popularity of this book is attested by numerous translations of it, and poetical versions of parts of it, which appeared in England and France, in Italy and Germany from the 11th century onward to the 15th, and some even so late as the 16th. An Anglo-Saxon translation early in the 11th century seems to have been the first; but already in the 8th century the Descensus had been the theme of an Anglo-Saxon poem, and from both portions of this book, the Passion-plays or Mysteries which were presented

---

* Ap Migne, Patrologiae Cursus, Series Latina, t. LXXI. (1858), coll. 171-2. Cp. T. C. Thilo, Codex Apocryphus, N. T. Lipsiae, 1832, prolegg. pp. 118, 119, 121; Tischendorf, Evangelia Apocrypha Lipsiae, 1853, & 1876, prolegg. pp. 60, 61; R. A. Lipsius, Die Pilatus Acten Kiel, 1871, pp. 1, 4, 11.

† See Thilo, ll. prolegg. pp. 119, 120; Tischendorf, ll. prolegg. pp. 55-60; Lipsius, ll. pp. 1, 7-11; Wülcker, Das Evangelium Nicodemi U.S.W. Paderborn, 1872, p. 11.

so often in the 12th and 13th centuries, including the one which is still so successfully acted at Ober Ammergau, have derived some of their scenes.*

There are two recensions of the Greek text of the Gesta which differ very little in the narrative, except that one, probably the older version, is more concise than the other. The longer account is introduced by a prologue, written in the name of Ananias or Aenias, apparently a Christian Jew, who states that he sought and found the account which had been written, shortly after the crucifixion of our Lord, by Nicodemus in Hebrew, and that he himself translated it into Greek in the 17th year of Flavius Theodosius and the 5th of his Colleague Valentinian. This prologue is attached to the Latin version also; but several of the MSS. commence with the statement that the book was found by the Emperor Theodosius at Jerusalem in the praetorium of Pontius Pilate. In another prologue Aenias is the author of the Hebrew original and Nicodemus, the Roman Toparch, translates it into Latin.†

As regards Joseph and Nicodemus, what is recorded of them in the Gesta may be comprised in a few words. The interposition of the two friends on behalf of the accused Prophet, and the reverence they had shown for him in his burial, drew down upon them the wrath of the Jewish rulers. They were afraid to arrest Nicodemus, as he was a ruler in Israel, and a man of great influence, but they seized Joseph and shut him up in a strong cell or dungeon, which was closely guarded, purposing to put him to death after the Sabbath day should have closed. Joseph in his dungeon spent the night and the fol-

---

* Notes, Note 3.

† See Thilo, ll. prolegg. pp. 121, 124-36, 139, also 150, 158; Tischendorf, ll. prolegg. pp. 57-61; Lipsius, ll. pp. 4, 5, 7, 8, 11, 12, 13; Wülcker, ll. pp. 28, 30, 98.

lowing day in prayer; and at midnight the house was lifted up by the four corners, a brightness as of lightning shone around him, and his Lord, now risen, appeared to him, saying to him, "Fear not, Joseph! I am Jesus," and led him forth, first to the empty tomb, and then to his own house in Arimathea. There he was charged to remain closely within doors for forty days.

Next day the Jews found that they were baffled at all points. When they sent for their prisoner he had disappeared, though the doors were still sealed and firmly closed, and the Roman guards of the now empty sepulchre came to tell them of the great earthquake, and of the angel who had rolled away the stone, and had announced to the women who were waiting there that Jesus was risen from the dead, and that His disciples would find Him in Galilee. When they refused to believe, the soldiers, who had heard of the escape of Joseph, tauntingly challenged them to produce him, if they required them to produce Jesus. After a time messengers came from Galilee, reporting that Jesus had been seen there with His disciples, and it was found that Joseph was at his own house in Arimathea. So the chief priests and the rulers, being in great anxiety and alarm, sent messengers with an apologetic letter to Joseph, entreating him with great deference to return to their Council. He returned to Jerusalem with the messengers, and was received by Nicodemus, who invited Annas and Caiaphas and the chief rulers of the Synagogue to meet him. When solemnly questioned by them, he told them how Jesus had visited him in the prison, had brought him out, and led him to the empty sepulchre. Joseph's audience is represented as greatly astonished at his story, some of them convinced, and in dismay at what they had been doing in their enmity to Jesus, but others still unwilling to believe. The next day they sat in Council, and examined the three men from Galilee, who testified that they had seen Christ after His Resurrection, and

THE HOLY GRAIL

had seen Him borne up in a cloud to Heaven.*

The Descensus is introduced by Joseph saying to Annas and Caiaphas in the Council that Jesus had not risen alone, but many of the dead had risen with Him, and among them had been recognised two sons of Simeon, who, as they all knew, had died shortly before. He advised that they should be found if possible, and questioned about the mystery of their resurrection; and as they had been seen in Arimathea, Annas, Caiaphas, and Gamaliel went there with Joseph and Nicodemus, found them, and persuaded them to come with them to Jerusalem, where they wrote their narrative in the Synagogue.†

An appendix of comparatively late origin, found in Latin copies of the *Evangelium Nicodemi*, states that Pilate, while preparing to make his official report of all these transactions to the Roman Emperor, extracted from the chief priests a full confession that the claim of Jesus to be the promised Messiah was well founded. They professed to have discovered this in examining their Sacred Writings, after they had received evidence of his Resurrection. The *duo testes*, whose testimony is particularly referred to, seem to be Leucius and Charinus.‡

The next group of documents which claims our attention is made up of a few pieces embracing the official correspondence, which has just been adverted to, and others narrating the sequel of Pilate's history, and also the dealings of the Roman Emperor with the Jews who were involved in the guilt of putting Jesus to death.

---

* See texts in Fabricius, ll. t.I. pp. 249-295; Thilo, ll. pp. 550-665; Tischendorf, ll. pp. 222-265, 275-300; 331-367.

† Tischendorf, ll. pp. 301-2, 368-371.

‡ See Fabricius, ll. t.I. pp. 295-7; Thilo, ll. pp. 789-795; Tischendorf, ll. pp. 388-391.

MEDIÆVAL LEGENDS

First we have surviving specimens of those despatches, said to have been sent to Rome by Pilate, which were fabricated early in the second century, and which are mentioned as current in their own time by Justin Martyr, Tertullian, Eusebius, and others.* They evince in their tone at once a penitential feeling, and a desire to propitiate the displeasure which the deed that they report might naturally provoke at Rome. One of them is the Ἀναφορὰ Πιλάτου or Pilate's Report, which, while it confesses in a few apologetic words his own weak compliance with the urgent demands of the Jews, is in reality a summary of the miracles of Christ, and of the portents that followed the Crucifixion. This is extant in Greek only. It is addressed in different copies to "Tiberius Caesar," to "Augustus Cæsar," and to "Tiberius Augustus."† Another is a separate epistle upon the same subject, represented by two quite distinct documents,‡ one of which is found only in late Latin MSS., and possesses no interest either in itself or in its history; but the other, though attached to the Gesta Pilati in Latin MSS. only, has been preserved also in the original Greek, being inserted entire in a celebrated Apocryphal work composed early in the second century, the *Acta Petri et Pauli*.§ The

---

* See Fabricius, ll. t.I. pp. 214-223; Thilo, ll. prolegg. pp. 118, 119; Tischendorf, ll. prolegg. pp. 62-4.; Lipsius, ll. pp. 14-20. In regard to Pilate's testimony to the miracles of Christ and His disciples, Eusebius is followed by (among others) Paul Orosius, Adv. Paganos Historiarum, l.VII., c. 4. He speaks of Pilate's suicide, ibid, c. 5.

† See Fabricius, ll. t.II. pp. 972-981, t.III. pp. 456-465; Thilo, ll. pp. 803-813; Tischendorf, ll. pp. 413-425, prolegg. pp. 77-8.

‡ See Fabricius, ll. t.I. pp. 298-301; coll. t.III. pp. 478-481; Thilo, ll. pp. 796-802, coll. prolegg. 136-7; Tischendorf, ll. pp. 392-5, 411-12, coll. prolegg. pp. 76-7.

§ This work is printed entire by Tischendorf, Acta Apostolorum

more recent fabrication is addressed, as was to be expected, to "Tiberius Cæsar," but the earlier epistle is superscribed to "Claudius," an anachronism which is surprising as coming from an author who wrote so soon after the events to which his narrative refers.*

The correspondence above described has its complement in a brief Greek narrative, the *Paradosis Pilatou*, "the Doom of Pilate."† This tells that the Emperor, full of horror and alarm, when he received from Jerusalem the report of the Crucifixion, and the darkness and the earthquake that followed it, ordered Pilate to be brought a prisoner to Rome, and in a public assembly, which was held in the temple of the gods, questioned him about the wonderful man whom he had given up to death. The Emperor then declared his conviction, from what Pilate had reported to him, that Jesus was the Christ, the King of the Jews.

As soon as the name of Christ was pronounced in the temple all the statues of the gods fell to the ground and became as dust, and the assembly dispersed in terror, every one to his own house. The Emperor then sent a charge to Licianus, one of his governors in the Eastern Provinces, to punish the guilty Jews, driving them from their country and dispersing them as slaves among other nations. Pilate was not excused for his share in the crime, but was condemned to be beheaded without delay.

He prepared for death, quietly and humbly, in prayer to Christ that He would mercifully forgive his sin, and be gracious to him, and also to Procla, his wife, who was standing by him in this hour of his death. "Thou didst open to her," he

---

Apocrypha, Lipsiae, 1851, pp. 1-39; the letter is in pp. 16-18.

* Notes, Note 4.

† Notes, Note 5.

said, "the prophetic vision of what was to come. Condemn her not for my sin, but grant to us both that we may be numbered with the righteous." As the prayer of Pilate was ended there came a voice from Heaven, blessing him, and announcing that "he should be seen as a witness for Christ at His Second Appearing, when He would come to judge the twelve tribes of Israel, and those that acknowledged not His name." Procla, his wife, hearing also the heavenly voice, died in an ecstasy of joy, and was buried with him.*

---

* See Thilo, ll. pp. 813-816; Tischendorf, ll. pp. 426-431, prolegg. pp. 78, 79.

CHAPTER III.

LATER LEGENDS EMBODIED IN LATIN DOCUMENTS.

IT is not worth while here to adduce any later references to the story of Joseph that may be found in Greek Hagiologies, Calendars, and Monastic Chronicles, No Latin documents, prior to the twelfth century, are known to be extant which treat of him separately, but his story continued during the previous centuries to be interwoven with the legends about Pilate and Veronica, legends in which both of these personages were associated with the Roman Emperor, and with the fate of Jerusalem.

The view expressed in the Paradosis, that Pilate became a true penitent, and died in the odour of sanctity, a view which has also been recognised in the Abyssinian Kalendar, was never accepted by the Latin Church; and hence most of the Western accounts present a gloomy picture of the Procurator, tortured by remorse in his last days, and perishing as a felon and a suicide.

Among the Latin texts in which these legends are preserved three are very prominent, each presenting distinctive features, and each being the prototype of numerous imitations and variations in prose and verse, some still composed in Latin, others translated into, or originally composed in, vernacular languages, especially French, German, and Anglo-Saxon.*

The first of these, being the oldest, simplest, and most fundamental of all, apparently belonging to the sixth or seventh century, is entitled *Mors Pilati*,† and runs parallel to

---

* Notes, Note 6.

† See Tischendorf, ll. pp. 432-435, coll. Prolegg, 79-80. Cp. Schön-

MEDIÆVAL LEGENDS

the Paradosis, but treats the subject independently, blending with it the legend of Veronica, and dilating upon the suicide of Pilate, the curse which rested upon his corpse, and its transportation to various localities in the South-East of Gallia, with one of which the writer himself appears to have been connected.

The second bears the title *Cura Sanitatis Tiberii Caesaris Augusti et Damnatio Pilati*, and devotes (as this title itself suggests) a much ampler space to the cure of the Emperor, by means of Veronica's relic, than to the exile and death of Pilate. Indeed it is obvious that the writer regarded the Veronica legend,—a favourite one in itself,—as here forming a pleasant contrast to the story of the ill-starred Procurator. This document was probably compiled in the seventh or eighth century. It has been repeatedly edited from MSS. of the eighth, ninth, and subsequent centuries, and it was summarised in the eleventh century by Marianus Scotus.*

The third is a compilation,—made apparently in Aquitania,—of the eighth century also, and we have an Anglo-Saxon version of it, as old at any rate as the beginning of the eleventh century. Its title, *Vindicta Salvatoris*, marks the principal theme and purpose of the composition. As it was the author's intention to signalise the sufferings of the Jews in the siege of Jerusalem, and the final dispersion of their nation by the Roman legions, as the just retribution for the crucifixion of Christ, he has subordinated to his full description of

---

bach, ll. pp., 170-173. The Mors Pilati is transcribed in the Legenda Aurea of Jacobus a Voragine, ed. Graesse, Lipsiae, 1850, cap. LIII, pp. 232-234; and is given in German in Das alte Passional.

* See Thilo, ll. prolegg., pp. 137-8; Tischendorf. ll. prolegg. pp. 81-3; and Shönbach, who has given the best edition of the text, ll. pp. 173-180.

THE HOLY GRAIL

this the legendary accounts of Pilate and Veronica, which are brought into the story in a clumsy and incoherent fashion.*

While these three documents, in so far as they occupy common ground, are animated by the same spirit, keep the same general outline of narrative, and even sometimes agree in minute details, they present also diversities more or less important. Alike in each of them Tiberius is reigning in Rome, and is suffering from a grievous malady. In the *Mors Pilati* and the *Cura Sanitatis*, the Emperor having heard of the Wonder-working Physician, who, as he thought, was still living in Judea, in the hope of being cured by him, despatches a trusty messenger to Pilate, with a request that he would at once send this great physician to Rome. In the *Vindicta Salvatoris* Tiberius, still Roman Emperor, only sends his messenger to Judæa when advised to do so by Titus and Vespasian, after they have already avenged the death of Christ. In all these narratives, as also in the later versions where Vespasian is the sick Emperor, Veronica and her relic are brought to Rome, and the cure is effected as soon as the sufferer looks on the likeness of Christ.

In the *Cura Sanitatis* and the *Vindicta*, Veronica is introduced as the Haemorrhousa of the Canonical Gospels (Mark v., 25-34), while nothing is said of this in the *Mors Pilati*. There is some variation also, even in different MSS. of the same composition, as to the way in which she obtained the likeness of Christ. In one of these versions she was going to a painter to have the portrait painted on a piece of linen, which

---

* See Tischendorf, ll. pp. 448-463, and prolegg. pp. 81-3; also Schönbach, pp. 183-6 The Anglo-Saxon version, entitled S. Veronix, with the initial fragment of another one is printed by C. W. Goodwin, Publications of the Cambridge Antiquarian Society, No. 1. Anglo-Saxon Legends of St. Andrew and St. Veronica, Cambridge, 1851, cp. 26-47, of Introduction, pp. 6-11.

MEDIÆVAL LEGENDS

she had procured for the purpose, when Christ met her, and knowing what she wished, He took the linen and impressed upon it the likeness of His face. According to one MS. of the *Cura Sanitatis*, she took the portrait herself, it is not clearly explained how, while another gives the story which has become the prevalent form of the legend, that Christ being wearied after a journey, this woman gave Him a napkin to wipe the sweat from His face, and that He returned it to her with his likeness imprinted upon it.*

As to Joseph and Nicodemus, the *Mors Pilati* has no mention of them at all. In the *Vindicta Salvatoris* they both appear before the Commissioner of Tiberius. Nicodemus testifies his belief in Christ as the Saviour of the world, and Joseph tells the story of his imprisonment, and his liberation by Christ, just as it is recorded in the *Gesta Pilati*. In the *Cura Sanitatis* that narrative is not repeated, and Joseph only gives his testimony as one of the disciples who saw and talked with Christ after His resurrection. The Anglo-Saxon version of the *Vindicta* takes an independent course in this, as in some other points. In it Joseph tells of his burial of Christ, of seeing the empty sepulchre, and the two angels, and of seeing Christ afterwards with His disciples "in the same flesh in which he was before."

As the legends noticed in this chapter have no further reference to the main subject of this Essay, the following pages, which discuss them more at length may be considered episodical, and Chapter IV. may be perused or passed over at the reader's discretion.

---

* Notes, Note 7.

CHAPTER IV.

Section I.

Discrepancies in the Latin Legends Concerning Pilate.

VERY little seems to have been known with certainty about the life of Pilate either before or after what we hear of him in the Gospels, so there was a wide field for imagination as to his career. As to his early life, the blank came to be filled with a very ingeniously invented story, as to his last years we find in these legendary writings a variety of conflicting statements.

In the *Vindicta Salvatoris* nothing is said of Pilate except that, after the Siege of Jerusalem, he was left in close imprisonment at Damascus. In the *Cura Sanitatis* he is brought a prisoner to Rome, and though his life is spared by Tiberius, he is deported to some place, not readily identified under the corrupt names assigned to it, though perhaps Ameria in Tuscia (=Umbria) is intended. There, according to one MS., he killed himself in the first year of Gaius (=Caligula). But most of the MSS. state that he survived until the reign of Nero, and that at the trial of SS. Peter and Paul, under that Emperor, not only was his letter to Claudius produced from the Archives and read before the Court, but he was himself recalled to Rome to give evidence as to the facts reported in it. It is added that on examination of his antecedents he was remitted to his place of banishment where he ended his miserable career by falling upon his own sword.

Of course in regard to the letter being read before Nero, this narrative rests upon the authority of the *Acta Petri et*

MEDIÆVAL LEGENDS

Pauli. As to the appearing of Pilate in person before the same Emperor, it has the concurrence, perhaps of some Latin copies of those *Acta,* but certainly of the *Chronographia* of Johannes Malalas, lx., pp. 328, 331 * (coll. Chronicon Alexandrinum, p. 580), though there Nero is said to have sentenced him not to exile but to death.

The *Mors Pilati* represents the Procurator as brought to Rome, after the Emperor's restoration to health, as subjected to repeated examinations, as finally doomed to death, and as committing suicide in prison. The Seamless Tunic of Christ is introduced, as worn by Pilate in his first interviews with the Emperor, and as operating like a spell upon Tiberius, forcing him against his will to be mild and gentle to the prisoner every time he came before him, till it was removed. The writer also expatiates on, and may be said to gloat over the indignities inflicted on the suicide's corpse, excluded from sepulture alike by man and by nature, by water and by land, and therefore transported from place to place, on its way from Rome and the bed of the Tiber to its final resting place among the Swiss Alps, in a gloomy tarn or in a rifted rock overhanging the water.

This gruesome story of Pilate's corpse, a plaything of evil spirits, and a plague and danger to men in all the places where it rested, had evidently a great fascination for the chroniclers of those early centuries. The numerous writers who have repeated the story have assigned various names to the mountainous tract where its migrations ended, such as *Mons Toritonius, Mons Septimus, Mons Fractus, Mons Tranchié.* The name *Mons Pilatus,* so familiar to us, whether altered or not from Pileatus="cloud-capped," and that of the storm-vexed tarn *Lacus Pilati* or *Puteus Pilali,* do not perhaps occur in writ-

---

* In L. Dindorf's edition, pp. 254, 256.

THE HOLY GRAIL

ings prior to the seventeenth century.* The intermediate localities specified in the *Mors Pilati* are Vienna (Allobrogum), known to the writer under an older name-form Vigenna, which he whimsically derives from *Via Gehennae*,† and Losania. In derivative compositions the names Vienne and Lausanne are generally accepted, but in some an inclination appears to substitute Lucerne for Lausanne, and for Vienne Lyon (Lugdunum), not to mention that one, a German version, substitutes Jenff (=Geneva). In a few pieces it is not the corpse that is transferred from the banks of the Tiber to those of the Rhone, but the living man, who passes his last days at Vienne or at Lyons, a miserable exile. The latter view has been accepted by several chroniclers of early date, who had perhaps learned from Josephus (Antt. Jud. xviii., 7, 2, xvii., 13, 2. Bel. Jud. ii., 9, 6.) that Herod Antipas, the associate of Pilate, was deported to Lyon, A.D. 39, and subsequently into Spain, and that his brother, Archelaus, had been some years before secluded in Vienne. At any rate Pilate is said by Abp. Ado, writing about A.D. 870, followed by Otto of Freisingen before A.D. 1146, to have been banished to Vienne, but by Petrus Comestor, about A.D. 1170, followed by Vincent of Beauvais (Spec. Hist. 1. viii., c. 124), to have had Lyon assigned to him as his place of exile.‡ Jacopo a Voragine, in his far-famed

---

* See Ed. du Meril, Poesies Populaires Latines du Moyen Age, Paris, 1847, pp., 356-7. Among other works cited by him is Jean du Choul, Pilati Montis in Gallia Descriptio, who, through some confusion, identifies this Mons Pilati along with its Puteus Pilati, with Mont Commène in the Pyrenees.

† Notes, Note 8.

‡ P. Comestor, Hist. Scholast. in Actus Apost. C. LIII., ap Migne, Patrol Lat. t cxcviii., col. 1680, "Deportatus est in exilium Lugdunum unde oriundus erat, ut ibi in opprobrium generis sui moreretur."

MEDIÆVAL LEGENDS

Legenda Aurea, has transcribed these different accounts of Pilate's fate, trying, with his usual deference to authority, to reconcile them as far as possible; but he evidently attaches much more weight to the "Historia Scholastica," the work of Peter Comestor, than to the "Historia Apocrypha," viz.: the *Mors Pilati*, leaving it to the judgment of his readers to decide whether the latter is to be accepted or rejected, He refers also to Eusebius and Beda, as saying nothing of Pilate's exile but stating only that he died by his own hand.

Section II

The Fate of Pilate and the Destruction of Jerusalem Associated in Aquitanian Legends.

So much for the discrepancies observable in these Latin Texts while occupying common ground. But when we step beyond this ground, we find in the *Vindicta Salvatoris*, and the pieces derived from it, novel characters and events introduced in a fashion that startles us by its incongruity. Tiberius is still present in unchallenged supremacy, but the foreground of the stage is occupied by two personages named Titus and Vespasianus, who sail from Galicia to Judaea at the head of a large force, all but exterminate the guilty inhabitants, and then report their proceedings to their Lord Paramount in Rome. Here we have the destruction of Jerusalem, which was looked upon as the historic retribution for the death of Christ, referred indeed to its real agents, the two first Flavian Emperors, but on the other hand placed under the reign of Tiberius,—to whom Titus and Vespasian, while carrying it out, are subordinate,—and thus taken out of its true place in history and antedated by a whole generation.*

The aim kept in view by the authors, in this group of compositions, was evidently to present the punishment of Pilate, and the punishment of the Jewish leaders by the Roman Government, as two acts in the same drama; but this unity of presentment was very unskilfully achieved. The writer of the *Vindicta Salvatoris* has merely pieced together two relations already in vogue, linking on the one, which concerned the cure of Tiberius and its concomitants, as a sequel or appendix to the other, which was occupied with the causes

---

* See Tischendorf, ll. pp. 448, 452-5. Cp. Schönbach, ll. pp. 183-6.

MEDIÆVAL LEGENDS

and results of the Jewish campaign of Vespasian and Titus. Aquitanian patriots may have deemed it allowable, though they had, as far as appears, no traditional warrant, to claim for their province the honour of having been a training ground for two leaders whose career was to culminate in Imperial sway; just as Spain and the Rhineland respectively were the provinces governed by Galba and Vitellius, when they were proclaimed by the legionaries and received from them the oath of allegiance. At any rate no difficulties about time or place, and no misgivings about verisimilitude shackled the writers who originated or circulated the Aquitanian story. According to it, Titus a Regulus holding sway under Tiberius in Burgidalla (the modern Bordeaux), had an interview with a Christian Israelite named Nathan who, while proceeding as an envoy from Judaea to Rome, had been driven by adverse winds far from his destination, and finally wrecked upon the inhospitable coast of the Bay of Biscay. Titus, who had been suffering from a dreadful disease in his face, was at once cured on professing his faith in the Divine power of the Saviour, whose beneficent miracles, and death on the cross Nathan had announced to him. Having taken a vow to avenge the great Prophet, Titus sent messengers to another military chief, Vespasian, urging him to cooperate with him. At the head of their conjoined forces the two carried out their unsparing crusade against the Jews, and then made their report to Tiberius, who sanctioned all that they had done, and, acting upon their suggestion, sent a mission to Judaea which resulted in the cure of his own leprosy, and in his conversion and baptism.*

It is noticeable that here no relationship of blood between the two *Duces* is recognised. They are merely confederates and neighbours in a distant quarter of the empire, and Titus,

---

* See Tischendorf, ll. pp. 448-463.

THE HOLY GRAIL

who acts as the superior, is represented as a vassal-king under Tiberius, in accordance with the feudal ideas of the middle ages. Conceptions fundamentally the same mark some of the numerous paraphrases or repetitions of the *Vindicta Salvatoris,* ranging from the tenth to the fifteenth centuries, which either were embodied in Monastic Chronicles, or were circulated separately, under such titles as *Pilatus, S. Veronica, Nathanis Legatio, Vaspasien, La Destruction de Jerusalem, La Vengeance de la Mort de Notre Seigneur.* * In two Anglo-Saxon versions, one of which is known to be not later than the tenth century, while the date of the other is less certain, a corrupt reading of the name Titus, viz.: *Tirus* or *Tyrus* has originated two novel suggestions. The former version represents that the Aquitanian prince (A. S. cyning) with whom Vespasian was associated in command (A. S. fyrdgemacan) while he was still a pagan was called Tyrus, but received the name Titus at baptism. The latter version goes more wildly astray, for it names the Aquitanian king, whom gratitude for his cure induces to undertake the expedition, Tyrus and it makes Titus and Vespasian, not only his associates in that and other warlike enterprises, but his brothers.† But in most versions of the story the shipwrecked missionary comes not to Titus, but to Vespasian, whose seat of Government is located south of the Pyrenees, in the province of Galatia or Galiscia, and it is he who has the cancerous disease, and is cured when he hears of the life and death of Christ.

A thorough correction of the anachronism we have been noticing, might seem at first sight to have been effected by one bold and decisive stroke, in a Latin poem on Pilate composed in the twelfth century. It tells of two Kings (Reges)

---

* Notes, Note 9.

† See A. Sax Legends, ll. pp. 26-47, and Introduction pp. 9-11.

MEDIÆVAL LEGENDS

reigning at the same time, Titus in Rome and Vespasian in the distant West, and makes no mention of Tiberius. While, however, the two Emperors here bear the names that were usually coupled with each other in legend as well as in history, it is by no means clear that the writer thought of correcting an error of previous narrations, or that he was conscious of taking any step in advance; for, though he has substituted the name Titus for that of Tiberius, he has simply transferred to Titus, without adaptation and without reserve, the incidents which had been associated with Tiberius by his precursors. In this poem Titus reigns in Rome, suffers from leprosy, sends a mission to Judaea, is visited and cured by Veronica, and is advised as to the doom of Pilate by Vespasian who, after his own cure has come to Rome in order to confer with his colleague. The remainder of the poem is occupied with the fate of Pilate, and nothing is said of an expedition against the Jews. The date assigned to the conjoint reign, viz.: *post mortem Domini*, which appears to mean shortly after the Passion, bespeaks a misplacement as real, if not as glaring, as if Tiberius still occupied the throne.*

To the same twelfth century, and probably to an earlier portion of it, belongs a Latin-prose narrative concerning Pilate, which re-introduces Tiberius, but does not altogether commit itself to the error of the *Vindicta Salvatoris*. In this composition Vespasian is the Vassal-King in Galicia, and is cured in the same way as Titus was in the *Vindicta*. He also vows vengeance on the slayers of Christ, in case the Emperor should sanction an expedition against them; but we do not hear whether his intention was carried out. His part in the story stops short, and the rest of it is occupied with

---

* This Poem is printed entire by Ed. du Meril, ll. pp. 343-357. Cp. Schönbach, ll. pp. 194-5.

the cure of Tiberius through Veronica's relic, and the fate of Pilate. A French version of this narrative, composed early in the thirteenth century, adds a concise statement that the Prefect did obtain Caesar's assent, returned to his Spanish province and there proceeded to levy the forces with which he afterwards fulfilled his project.* In the *Legenda Aurea* (C. LXVII.), Vespasian is said to have had his petition granted while in Rome, to have then spent many years in *Monarchia Galatiae* assembling an adequate armament, and to have begun his campaign in Judaea in the time of Nero. This account is implicitly followed in a well-known German poem of the thirteenth century, *Das alte Passional;* and two other German poems of the same century, by Eike von Repgow and Gundacker von Judenborg respectively, harmonise with its tenor. In the one it is stated that the punishment of the Jews was resolved on by Tiberius, but not executed till the reign of Vespasian. The other tells how that often noticed letter, addressed by Pilate to Claudius was forwarded by the recipient to Nero, and how Nero, having been admonished by a celestial vision to avenge the death of Christ, commissioned Vespasian to proceed to Judaea for that purpose.† Here we have a combination of the old tradition, already cited from the *Cura Sanitatis*, that Pilate's letter to Claudius was publicly read in court before Nero, with the statement of Josephus, Suetonius, and other authorities that Nero, while in Achaia, despatched his ablest general Vespasian to Palestine, in order to crush a formidable rebellion against Roman supremacy in that province.

The well-read compiler of the *Legenda Aurea* has appealed to the testimony of Josephus, and admitted that it refers the

---

* See du Meril, ll. pp. 367-8. Cp. Schönbach, ll. pp. 195-6.

† See Schönbach, ll. pp. 197, 207, 205.

mission of Vespasian to the settled state policy of Rome, not to any surge of religious emotion in the mind of the reigning prince. But the Genoese Archbishop certainly held fast the theory of a grand Theodicy which included the fate of Pilate and the catastrophe of Jerusalem, nor could this conviction as to both events be at all affected by the lapse of a considerable period between them.

In regard to some other productions of the thirteenth and following centuries, it appears that chronological license, at all events, has been circumscribed by a growing acquaintance with authentic history, and by deference to its teachings, while they still reveal the influence of unverified legend in shaping their characteristic details. Let us take one specimen,—the French poem entitled *La Destruction* (or *La Prise*) *de Jerusalem*, preserved in MSS. of the thirteenth century. Here Tiberius—already left out in the Latin Pilate poem—does not reappear, and farther there is no mention of either a vassal-king or a prefect in Aquitania or in Galicia. Two Emperors, Vespasian the father, and Titus the son, reign conjointly in Rome, and both lead the crusading host against Jerusalem. But the echoes of the Tiberius legend are still distinctly audible. The elder Emperor is a victim to leprosy; but his Commissioner, now styled "Guy le Seneschal" instead of "Volusianus" or "Adrianus" brings over from Judaea Veronica and the marvellous portrait, by means of which he is at once cured. Afterwards, as it would seem, that favored votaress accompanies him and his son in their expedition to Palestine, both going and returning. Pilate is found, not only surviving, but still governing with vigour. To him, the zealots who defend the beleaguered city, look up as to their skilful and redoubted leader; and, after all is over, he is carried off to Rome among other distinguished captives. From Rome, according to this poem, he is sent to Vienne, "the place of banishment for State

THE HOLY GRAIL

criminals (criminels d'Etat)," and his end is made as terrible as words could paint it.* Similar narratives about the same personages form the warp and woof of two low German poems, composed probably in the fourteenth century.†

But before the last of these reproductions of the *Vindicta Salvatoris*—all of which ended with the tragic fate of Jerusalem,—had been composed, a legend, of a very different kind, had been taken up by writers who imparted to it a spiritual meaning, and an elevation of tone, which raised it above the bounds of place and time, and made it, in its essential idea, a symbol of the most sacred mysteries, and the highest aspirations of the Christian Faith. Though its real meaning soon became obscured and almost lost, under a mass of incongruous inventions, there still remained enough of the original idea in the Graal Romances to preserve for them a charm, and a halo of sacredness, which have survived from the twelfth century to the present day.

---

* See *Histoire Littéraire de la France*, t xxii., pp. 412-416; Ed. du Meril, ll. p. 357 Note; Schönbach, ll. pp. 197-8.

† See Schönbach, ll. pp. 202, y; 206-7, i.

CHAPTER V.

Joseph and Nicodemus in Judea.

AFTER reporting (in our second chapter) the most notable incidents which, in those ancient Graeco-Latin documents grouped under the heading of *Pilati Gesta*, are said to have followed the sepulture of Christ, we have been led to give an account of some later narratives in Latin, written and widely circulated in Western Europe between the sixth and tenth centuries, as continuations of the earlier legends. But we have found in these nothing further about Joseph and Nicodemus, except that, in the *Vindicta Salvatoris*, and in the *Cura Sanitatis Tiberii Caesaris*, they both appear among the witnesses examined by the Commissioner of Tiberius. In the *Cura Sanitatis* they both testify that they saw Jesus after His resurrection, and in the *Vindicta* Joseph repeats the story of his imprisonment by the Jews,—as it is told in the *Gesta Pilati*,—of Christ visiting him in the prison, releasing him, and leading him to the empty sepulchre.

Legends in Latin prose or verse concerning Joseph and Nicodemus, approximate in age and analogous in style to the *Vitae Pilati* metrical and prose, and the other compositions that we have noticed, were probably for a time in vogue, but, if still extant, they wait to be disinterred from Monastic libraries. We have redactions of the Joseph legend, in French prose and verse, claiming on valid grounds to be translated from, or based upon, Latin originals, analogous to *La Destruction de Jerusalem*, and other vernacular pieces indebted to the *Vindicta Salvatoris* and its variations; but these redactions belong to the twelfth century, and it has not been shown by crucial tests that their Latin originals were very much earlier. Our specimens of the Latin legend preserved in the archives

THE HOLY GRAIL

of Glastonbury have been transmitted by writers of the same century, such as William of Malmesbury and his followers; and both these sets of documents, especially the French compositions, luxuriate in descriptions of migrations and adventures, which mark the tastes of the crusading period more emphatically than those of any anterior age; though, so long as they occupy common ground with the documents that have been already reviewed, they present no modernisms in thought, or style, or imagery.

The part that Joseph of Arimathaea fills, in the French Romances of the *Saint Graal*, was evidently suggested by the story of Christ's visit to him in his imprisonment, given in the *Gesta Pilati*; but, in the Graal legend, Christ does not lead him out of the prison, but bids him remain there patiently for a time, and he is not delivered till the Roman Emperor comes to Jerusalem, to take vengeance on the Jews. This version of the story has its claim upon our attention strengthened by the fact that it has been inserted in the *Legenda Aurea*, with only such variations as show the author of that work to have drawn from an independent source. After describing the terrible sufferings of the Jews in the siege of Jerusalem, Jacobus a Voragine adds the following compendious statement:—"We read also that Titus, while entering Jerusalem observed a wall of great thickness, and ordered a breach to be made in it. This being done, there was found within an old man with hoary hair, and of venerable aspect, who, on being asked who he was, replied that he was Joseph of Arimathaea, a town of Judea, and that he had been closely immured there by the Jews on account of his having buried Christ. He added that from that time till the present, he had been sustained by celestial food and cheered by divine light."* Jacobus a Voragine refers also

---

* See the *Legenda Aurea*, ll. cap. LXVII., p. 302. The same account,

MEDIÆVAL LEGENDS

to the story of Joseph's release in the Gospel of Nicodemus, and suggests that the different accounts may be reconcileable, that he may have been imprisoned a second time by the Jews, because, after his release, he persevered in his testimony to Christ. The Archbishop of Genoa, who was born in 1230, could not have compiled the *Legenda Aurea* till far on in the thirteenth century, long therefore after several of the Graal Romances had been written, though only a faint report of the legend seems to have reached him.

In the oldest and simplest French redaction, the poem of Robert de Borron,—closely followed in its essential features by the elaborate romances which were composed shortly afterwards,—the story, when disengaged from a mass of theological teaching, is to this effect:—On the solicitation of his trusty adherent Joseph, who had long without payment rendered him knightly service, Pilate, who had most reluctantly authorised what he felt to be a judicial murder, permitted him and Nicodemus to take down from the cross, and inter the body of Jesus Christ, and also handed over to him a vessel (*veissel*) which had been brought to his palace by a Jew, from the house of Simon. It was the dish in which our Lord "made his sacrament" at the Last Supper with His disciples. In this vessel Joseph preserved the blood, which he washed from the five crucifixion wounds, and put it away carefully in his house at Arimathaea.

After the resurrection, the Jewish rulers, in their dismay at hearing the report of the guards, accused Joseph of stealing the body of Christ, seized him and hurried him away, cast-

---

in a form somewhat expanded, appears in the Catalogus Sanctorum of Petrus de Natalibus (concluded in 1372), lib. IV., cap. 2, cited by Bivar, ad Dextri Chronicon, A.D. 48, in Migne, ll. t. XXXI., p. 155.

ing him into a deep and darksome vault in a strong tower belonging to Caiaphas, where they left him to perish. But he was not forgotten by his Divine Friend, who very soon came to comfort him in his imprisonment. He did not then lead him forth, but exhorted him to abide patiently for a season, and left with him that doubly consecrated vessel, which was not only to supply him with sustenance, and irradiate his cell, but also to be a sign, and seal, and channel of divine grace.*

The interview between the prisoner and his newly-risen Saviour is very touchingly described; and indeed the whole spirit of this first part of Robert de Borron's work, "*Le Joseph d'Arimathie,*" as it is sometimes named, is in harmony with the character ascribed to its hero, "Le gentil cevalier, ki moult était piteus et dous, et de grand relegyon,"—gentle and reverent, full of kindliness and sympathy.

Thus Joseph's confinement commenced in the nineteenth year of the reign of Tiberius. Forty-two years afterwards, when the successors of that Emperor, Gaius, Claudius, and Nero had all passed away, Titus was upon the throne, and Vespasian, who, in all the documents with which we are now concerned, is treated as the son of Titus, is stated to have been long secluded from society by reason of a loathsome leprosy, but to have been cured by the sight of the marvellous portrait, which Veronica had been induced by the imperial Commissioners to bring to Rome. The Prince, grateful for his recovery, set out for Judea, accompanied by his father, to avenge the death of his Benefactor. Being informed that the body of Christ, when last seen, had been in the custody of Joseph of Arimathaea, he, aided by the Procurator, Pilate (though some other versions of the story name Pilate's successor, Felix), set afoot an enquiry as to the mysterious disappearance of that eminent Decurion,

---

* Notes, Note 10.

MEDIÆVAL LEGENDS

who had been so long sequestered that his very existence was forgotten by the outside world. The secret having been disclosed by one of the very few who were in possession of it, (Caiaphas is specially named), the prisoner was found still living, and was brought out by Vespasian himself, to whom he told his tale, still appearing as hale and vigorous as before he was cast into the dungeon.*

Joseph obtained from Vespasian pardon and safety for all the Jews who would believe in "the Holy Trinity, in Father, Son, and Holy Spirit," and a great company joined him, among whom were a surviving sister and her husband Hebron (more generally named Brons), with their twelve sons. He soon took leave of Vespasian, and led forth his numerous kinsmen and adherents into foreign and strange lands (en lointeinnes terres), where they abode for a long time.†

In this earliest version of the Graal legend Joseph does not cross the sea to Great Britain. The route he takes with his company, appears to be overland, and towards the East. Afterwards under divine direction they separate. Two parties, under their respective chiefs, directing their course to the distant West, "en la terre vers Occident." Joseph, having committed the Sacred Vessel to Brons, remains behind, forewarned that his life was soon to close.

"Et tu, quant tout ce feit aras,
Dou siècle te departiras."‡

---

* See *Le Roman du Saint Graal*, publié par Fr. Michel, Bordeaux, 1841, pp. 19-99; *Le Saint Graal*, publié par E. Hucher, Paris, 1875. Tome I., pp. 209-333.

† See *Le Roman du Saint Graal*, ll. pp. 97, vv. 2296-9; p. 99, vv. 2361-4.

‡ See *Le Roman du Saint Graal* ll. p. 143, vv. 3395-6.

Here we find a variation, for the metrical redaction, and most MSS. of the prose one, import that he returned to "the land where he was born," and died there, while a single MS. in prose says that he remained in the land to which he had been sent: "*Ensinc remest Joseph et fina en la terre et oú päis où il fu envoiez de par Jhésu Christ.*" The writer of this MS. has specified, among the distant countries embraced in Joseph's mission, "*la grande Bretaigne.*" He seems to have taken this statement from the later Romance, "*Le grand Saint Graal*," which ascribes the conversion of Great Britain to Joseph.*

A statement implying the sepulture of Joseph in, or near Jerusalem, was, at all events, accepted at the beginning of the ninth century, in the later years of Charlemagne; for at that time Fortunatus of Grado is said to have visited the Holy City, and to have brought from it various precious relics of saints, and among them the body of Joseph, which he bequeathed to the monastery of Moienmoutier in the Vosges, of which he had been elected Abbot.†‡

In the traditions which ignore the legend of Joseph's imprisonment, and his miraculous release, he is not marked out from his fellow disciples for any signal achievement, but remains devoutly subject to apostolic rule and teaching, aiding his fathers and brethren in Christian work within his own land or in foreign countries. In the accounts which represent him and Nicodemus as working together on equal terms without interruption, a difference is observable, which at first sight appears to be of slight moment, but which becomes more significant in the light of later developments. It concerns the

---

* See E. Hucher, ll. Tome I., pp. 262, 265, 275.

† Richer of Senones (early in the thirteenth century) Chronicon, Lib II., cap. 6; quoted by M. Paulin Paris, Romania, t.I.

‡ Notes, Note 11.

MEDIÆVAL LEGENDS

particular Apostles to whom they were respectively indebted for pastoral care. Nicodemus is said to have been a catechumen of SS. Peter and John,—obviously because those two are usually associated in the canonical Gospels and Acts,—Joseph is represented as receiving baptism and instruction from SS. Philip and John, as co-operating with them in their ministry, and especially in their cares for the Virgin Mother, at whose "Dormition" he was permitted to be present. In some forms of the tradition the name of St. John has been replaced by that of St. James the Just, and this naturally enough, since his episcopal authority was generally associated with the city and vicinity of Jerusalem. The coupling of Philip and John was doubtless suggested by the celebrated tradition, traceable to the latter part of the second century, that the Apostolic College partitioned among its members, two by two, the provinces which were to be immediately evangelized, and that Asia Minor with Achaia, was assigned either to Philip and Bartholomew, or to Philip and John, as the sphere of their labours.* It would seem to have been assumed, in the course of time, that Philip was likely to co-operate, as with John in the North-West, so with St. James the Just, in superintending missionary operations in Syria and Palestine. It may be remarked here that the prominent part assigned to him, in initiating and directing missionary enterprises, would be not unnaturally suggested, partly by various incidents which are recorded about him in the Canonical Gospels, partly also by a confusion between him and his namesake, the Deacon and Evangelist, which crept into traditions of the Church as early as the second and third centuries. We read of the latter Philip preaching the Gospel with success to the Samaritans, to the Aethiopian minister, and to the Philistines of Azotus on his

---

* Notes, Note 12.

THE HOLY GRAIL

way to Caesarea; and in that prominent seat of government and great commercial haven he took up his abode, and kept an open house for the Christians who passed through it.*

It was almost to be expected that the Apostle Philip should be, in some legends, represented as prosecuting his mission work on the Phoenician sea-board, and thence despatching messengers of salvation to the most distant realms of the West,—and perhaps accompanying them, and for a time taking part in their work. Eastern accounts tell only of his mission to Asia Minor, and his death and burial at Hierapolis; but there was a tradition in early times, supported by Isidore of Seville, and Freculphus of Fulda, that Philip the Apostle visited the Gauls, and "brought to the light of the gospel, and the haven of faith, the barbarians dwelling in darkness by the swelling ocean." And if he did not himself cross the Channel to Britain, it may well be believed,—as is suggested by William of Malmesbury,—that he imparted light to this side also, by sending over some of his missionary band, and, as their leader, Joseph of Arimathaea whom the Monks of Glastonbury have claimed as the founder of their monastery, and the builder of the first Christian Church that was erected in Britain.†

With regard to Nicodemus, various extant traditions are in favour of the view that after the Ascension, he passed the remainder of his days in his own country, an avowed believer in Christ. For this we have vouchers, clearer and more direct

---

* Acts VIII., 5·13, 26-40, XXI., 8-10.

† "Philippus Gallis praedicat Christum, barbaras gentes vicinasque tenebris et tumenti Oceano conjunctas ad scientiae lumen fideique portum deducit. Ysidorus in Libro de Vita et Ortu et Obitu Sanctorum." Legenda Aurea, cap. LXV., p. 292. Wm. of Malmesbury, Chronicles of the Kings of England, Ed. J. A. Giles, p. 21, London, 1847.

MEDIÆVAL LEGENDS

than certain Talmudic statements (which by the way involve a chronological discrepancy similar to those which have been remarked in the Pilate legends), regarding a pious Pharisee, Bonai, the son, or (as has been suggested) the father of Gorion, who is said to have acquired in addition to his original name that of Nicodemus.* A narrative proceeding from Chrysippos, a Presbyter of Jerusalem in the fifth century, and repeated by many early and grave authorities, is to the effect that our Nicodemus, expelled from the Sanhedrim, and from the city, as a convert to Christianity, retired to the country house of his kinsman Gamaliel, and that both of them, with Gamaliel's son Abibos (perhaps for Aquiba) who was likewise converted, were there buried in adjacent tombs. It is true that, in all the accounts, St. Stephen is represented as having been previously interred in the same vault, and the body of Nicodemus is said to have been laid at his feet. It is true also that the record of the three Rabbin has paled in the surpassing lustre of the Greek Proto-Martyr; but still the names of all the four are everywhere preserved as co-partners in the tomb, and it is Gamaliel who is said to have appeared in a vision to the local Presbyter, A.D., 415, and revealed to him their common place of sepulture.† The frequent translation, in the course of ages, of St. Stephen's remains to Jerusalem, Constantinople, Rome, and various other places in Europe, and in Africa, has been

---

* See (besides earlier authorities) J. C. Wolfius, Bibliotheca Hebraea, Part (Hamburgi, 1721), pp. 583-4; J. H. Otho, Lexicon Rabinico-Philologricum (Altona, 1757), pp. 459-60; S. R. Paulus in Joannem III. 1; Thilo, ll., p. 550.

† See Photius Bibliotheca, Cod. 171, p. 118, ed. Bekker; Lukianus Presbyter, Epistola ap. S. Augustin. Opera, ed. Bened. t. VII., Appendice; J. a Voragine, Legenda Aurea, cap. CXII., pp. 461-2; Breviarium Romanum, Augusti die III., p. 522, Bellovaci et Dublini, 1861.

THE HOLY GRAIL

reported by Church Historians and Doctors.* The shadow of his renown may perhaps account for the absence of any mention of simultaneous translations of the relics which were at first associated with his.

The citizens of Pisa, as is well known, brought over in their argosies, in the twelfth century, from Calvary, the earth which forms their Campo Santo. They assert that they acquired also, about A.D. 1100, the relics of Nicodemus and his two kinsmen, presented to them by Godfrey of Bouillon, as a reward for their services. It is desirable that they should have some evidence of older date than an altar preserved in the Cathedral, of Cinque Cento style, inscribed with the names of the three Saints, with an epitaph in twenty bad elegiacs upon a suspended tablet.† It is probable that some relics of these saints were claimed also for the old church of St. Nicodème in the Armorican district of Morbihan, the modern representative of which, erected in the sixteenth century, contains shrines dedicated to them, in which stand their effigies grim and swarthy.‡

At variance with the traditions which assigned separate careers to Joseph and Nicodemus, is a belief, which was perhaps prevalent in early times, though no early testimony to it has been adduced, that the two friends, closely linked in their lives and in death not long divided, found repose together, a few feet apart, in graves adjacent to the tomb in which they had laid their Lord; not indeed beneath the floor, at the spot pointed out by modern guides, but in excavations cut out of

---

* Notes, Note 13.

† The altar inscription and the tablet were published by J. C. Wagenseil, Sota, Altdorf, 1574, pp. 992-3. Cp. Murray's Handbook of Central Italy, 1875, p. 144.

‡ See the description in Temple Bar, vol. 46, No. 184, pp. 386-391.

MEDIÆVAL LEGENDS

the rock in the rear, in which recent criticism has found confirmation of the tradition that the church built by Constantine really encloses an ancient Judaic burial place—perhaps the very sepulchre around which the associations of both Eastern and Western Churches still fondly linger.*

---

* See Lord Nugent, Lands Classical and Sacred, vol. II., pp. 33-45; A. P. Stanley, Sinai and Palestine, pp. 457-8, 465.

CHAPTER VI.

Migrations from Palestine to Western Europe in the Apostolic Age.

WE have already had occasion to remark that, in those versions of the Joseph legend which ignored his custody of a Sacred Vessel that was a source of nutriment, and of spiritual light, he is represented as continuing to enjoy apostolic direction, but as originating no policy of his own, and as exhibiting no traits of individual character. So likewise the migrations conducted by him or his kinsmen, in the accounts of which the presence and influence of that Sacred Vessel are passed by in silence, cannot be said to differ in class, or in their main outlines from other migrations referred to the same early period, to which various communities throughout Western Europe were accustomed to trace back the foundation of their own National Christianity.

In the rivalry which turned, not upon the question which of them had most purely and efficiently carried out the precepts of their common faith, but upon the relative antiquity of the missions by which the gospel had been first announced within their borders, the priority of Rome in this regard, as well as in most others, was generally admitted, even by the ambitious Gallic and Belgic cities which long nourished a jealousy of the all-embracing influence of the Latin capital. From the time when Rome was believed to enclose the tombs and the actual bones of St. Peter, as well as of St. Paul, she stood in this respect beyond competition. But an approximation to her pre-eminence came to be essayed in the Western Provinces, some of which alleged that they likewise had been visited and instructed by some member of the Apostolic College,

MEDIÆVAL LEGENDS

while others were fain to attach themselves to the skirts of voyagers whose highest distinction was that they had been companions of the Apostles.

As to these missionary visits, we find a marked distinction in the area, and the duration of the influence that tradition has ascribed to some of them in comparison with others. Some are only mentioned as cursory visits, effecting their purpose at the time, but leaving no abiding memorials. In connection with several of the Apostles, as well as with persons of less distinction, surmises were from time to time thrown out which originated scholastic theories, but failed to grow up into national beliefs. Quite different were the traditions which came to be widely accepted, and to hold a permanent place, respecting such missionaries as were in course of time looked up to as the Tutelars of large communities, provinces, and nations, being regarded as the founders of famous religious establishments where their supulchres sanctified the soil and attracted hosts of reverent pilgrims from far and near.

Section I

Legends about the Apostles James and Philip in Spain and Gaul.

This distinction is conspicuous in the course and issues of the oldest Western legend regarding the advent of two Apostles, James the son of Zabdiah, and Philip of Bethsaida, a legend which was early embodied in an occidental, and specially a Spanish version of the story of the allotment of the known world as a mission field among the twelve apostles. The desire which sprung up in the Western provinces of the Empire, to find themselves included in the Apostolic Chart, prompted at least one attempt to accommodate that old story to local requirements.

In a treatise entitled *De Ortu et Obitu Patrum*, which was at one time groundlessly attributed to S. Hieronymus, but which a mass of evidence shows to have been composed by S. Isidore of Seville, who died A.D. 636, it is stated (c. 81) that the provinces assigned severally to the Apostles were these:—to Peter, Rome; to Andrew, Achaia; to James, Spain; to Thomas, India; to John, Asia; to Andrew, Macedonia; to Philip, Gaul; to Bartholomew, Sycaonia; to Simon Zelotes, Egypt; to Matthias, Judaea; to James, the Lord's brother, Jerusalem; to Jude, the brother of James, Mesopotamia. This passage, with the exception of the last clause, has been transcribed in a common-place book, erroneously attributed to the Venerable Beda, who died, A.D. 735, and also, without any variation, in the Chronicon of Freculphus, Abbot of Fulda, finished before A.D. 851, (Tom. ii., Lib. ii., cap. 4); while it has been cited or appealed to by numerous Spanish writers, beginning perhaps with Julian, Abp. of Toledo, in the seventh

MEDIÆVAL LEGENDS

century. There is also in the Mosarabic Liturgy a hymn, probably by S. Hildefonsus, a hearer of Isidore, who died A.D. 667, to much the same effect, which assigns Gaul to Philip, to John Boanerges, Asia, and to his brother James, Spain. Further, Isidore, in two distinct paragraghs of the treatise mentioned above, relates (c. 71) that James, son of Zebidaeus, preached the gospel in Spain, and in adjacent countries in the West, and on returning to his own land was slain by Herod the Tetrarch, and was buried in a marble sarcophagus, and (c. 73) that Philip imparted the light of the gospel to the Gauls and the Barbarians bordering on the outer ocean, and that he finally suffered martyrdom in the Phrygian Hierapolis. The passage about Philip is quoted from Freculphus by William of Malmesbury, in the twelfth century, and from Isidore by Jacobus a Voragine in the thirteenth.* Both of the passages have been closely followed in various later works, such as our English *Cursor Mundi* of the fourteenth century (vss. 21009-21018, and vss. 21079-21088).

But the account of the Partition given, under A.D. 34, in the Chronicon which bears the name, and was intended to pass for the work of Flavius Lucius Dexter, about A.D. 440 (though it was really vamped up, probably by Geronimo Romano da Higuera, shortly before A.D. 1400), while still assigning Spain to James the Greater, represents Philip as having had *Scythia et Galliæ* allotted to him. Here we have a notable interpolation, obviously designed to harmonise the Isidorian version of the legend with another account which the chronicler knew to have had extensive circulation. This account is set forth in some Latin hexameters which have been ascribed to writers, widely even ludicrously separated in locality and date,—to

---

* William of Malmesbury, Chronicle of the Kings of England. Ed. J. A. Giles, 1847, p. 21; Legenda Aurea, ll. c. LXV., p. 292.

THE HOLY GRAIL

Venantius Fortunatus, Bishop of Poitou in the sixth century; to Aldhelm, Abbot of Malmesbury, in the seventh; to Aleuin of York, afterwards Abbot of St. Martin at Tours, in the eighth; and to Walafrid Strabo, Abbot of Reichenau, in the ninth. These hexameters are divided into thirteen portions, which were intended to be inscribed on the altars of the Virgin and the twelve Apostles within a Church, which a poem, incorporated with them in one MS., represents as built while Ini reigned in Wessex. The portion relating to St. James commemorates the conversion of Spain accomplished by him, previously to his martyrdom under Herod the Tetrarch; but the portion devoted to Philip signalizes that Apostle as converting the barbarous tribes of Scythia, and thence proceeding into Asia which he evangelized, and where he died and was entombed.

No connection formed by either Apostle with any foreign country is mentioned in any of the older Latin *Martyrologia*,—that which passes under the name of Hieronymus, the so-called "Old (or shorter) Roman" one, that of Beda, with the additions by Florus of Lyons, about A.D. 830, that of Rabanns Maurus of Fulda, about A.D. 845, that of Ado of Vienne and Lyons, about A.D. 858. But in a kindred, perhaps a later treatise, the same Ado states, as to James the son of Zebedee, that he was beheaded by Herod, and that his bones were translated to the furthest limits of Spain over against the British sea, and there continue to be deeply venerated; and as to Philip, that after converting almost all Scythia, he returned into Asia, and was buried at Hierapolis. These statements regarding both Apostles have been repeated in substance by Usuard of St. Germain at Paris, about A.D. 875, while Usuard's younger contemporary, Notker Balbulus of St. Gall, has copied closely Ado's expresssions, adding, as a reason for the translation of James's bones, that the Spaniards were said to have been converted by him during his life.

MEDIÆVAL LEGENDS

The idea of uniting Gallia and Scythia, so as to reconcile the varying accounts of the Apostle Philip's journeyings, was no doubt suggested by the belief, which is favoured by the language of the chroniclers and martyrologists above referred to, that the "Scythia" of those accounts extended far over Europe, and might be conceived as bordering on, or even including, Gallia in the remotest West. So in the more numerous notices which specify "Scythia" as evangelized by the Apostle Andrew, that region is treated as stretching over a great part of Europe, so that at last it was supposed to embrace the home of the Picts and Scots, and its very name was recognised in that of "Scotia" as merely a later variant of it. Such expressions as "Celto-Scythae" and "Scythia-Europæ" denote the extension of a previously limited term over the Western Continent, as the phrases "Indo-Scythae," "Scythia intra Imaum," "Scythia extra Imaum," show how far it reached over the Asiatic Continent. And on both sides we are reminded of the fact that "Scythia" is the vaguest of all geographical designations, as "Scyth" is the vaguest of all that are employed in ethnography.

A reconciliation however, if considered desirable, might be effected by means of a very different hypothesis; though the claims of the Western Nations to direct communion with the Apostles would be thereby seriously damaged. In the Latin work *Historia Certaminis Apostolorum*, compiled about A.D. 910, though claiming for its author Abdias, Bishop of Babylon in the first century, Philip is said to have "passed twenty years in Scythia," converting the scattered hordes, and thence to have "returned into Asia," where he died at an advanced age, and was buried at Hierapolis. Here the application of the term "Scythia" is very uncertain, and "Asia" may denote either Asia Minor in general, or, in accordance with the later usage, the Pro-consular Province of which Ephesus was the capital. In the very ancient apocryphal tract *Acta Philippi*, the Apostle is spoken of as journeying through the cities of "Lydia and Asia," (for which names in one of the derivative accounts "Lydia and Mysia" are substituted), and as put to death in "Hierapolis of Asia." Here of course "Asia" signifies the Proconsular Province, specially its Phrygian division. In this account "Scythia" is not mentioned at all. In the analogous Greek *Acta Andreæ*, are related the sufferings, miracles and successes of that Apostle in the city (or community) of the Anthropophagi, and the subsequent mission of him and his brother Peter into the city (or community) of the Barbari. The narrative of Abdias (Lib. iii.), substitutes for Anthropophagi the fanciful name Myrmidones,* and mentions Nicaea and Nicomedia among the places which Andrew afterwards visited.

The same transactions with various others are rehearsed in the *Acta Andreæ* of Epiphanius, a Monk of Jerusalem in the eleventh or twelfth century, drawn from various authorities both early and late. In this strange jumble several accounts of the travels of the Apostle follow each other in a disorderly series, some of which are mere repetitions of others, some follow what they ought to precede, and some violate all geographical conditions. However, the localities specified are so numerous that they help to define the more vague notices which we have reported from previous documents. Thus Andrew is said to have been "called away to visit Scythia," with the result that "he went down to Sinope, a city of Pontus among the tribes called Scyths." He is found also visiting Iberia, the banks of the Phasis, the Lazi, Zecchi, Alani, Sogdaei, Pontus, Paphlagonia, Bithynia, Galatia, Phrygia, Mysia and Lydia: and among the

---

* Ap. Fabricius. Cod. Apoer. N.T. t.I. p. 457. A compromise between the two readings is suggested by Nicephorus, H.E. c. 41, who gives "Myrmene" as situated in the country of the Anthropophagi.

towns are distinguished Sinope in Pontus (this being apparently the "city of the Anthropophagi" in the Apocryphal Acta), Trapezus, Amisus, Amasia, Amastris, Heraclea, Nicomedia, Nicaea, Chalcedon, Ephesus, Laodicea,—all before the Apostle crossed the Thracian Bosphorus. Here obviously "Scythia" is located to the South East and East of the Black Sea,* while here, as well as in the superscription of Peter's first Epistle, "Galatia" is the country occupied by those *Galatæ* who had re-emigrated from Europe in the third century B.C., had intermingled with the Greek residents and learned their language, and had been favoured with two visits and a pastoral letter from St. Paul. Now it is highly probable that in some Greek notices regarding St. Philip "Galatia" and "Scythia" were employed in the same sense, but were misunderstood by Isidore and other Western writers, who being aware that "Galatia" was the Greek name for Gallia, and that "Scythia" was a very elastic term, were thus led to transfer that Apostle's adventures from the shores of the Euxine to those of the Atlantic. But this surmise, whether well or ill founded, is widely different from the conjecture that even in the Isidorian texts "Gallia" is a corrupt lection and should be replaced by "Galatia," a conjecture which has been justly repudiated, since it is as clear that Isidore with his followers wrote, and intended to write, "Gallia" as it is that they wrote and intended to write "Hispania." In the second Epistle to Timothy, iv, 10, a reading "Gallia" instead of Galatia is presented in some MSS., versions and Fathers, but it, as well as the reference which it implies,

---

* On Scythia in this connexion cp. R. A. Lipsius, *Die Apokryphen Apostelgeschichten und Apostellegenden*, Braunschweig, 1883-1887, and Wiltsch Geography of the Church, London, 1868, vol. I., p. 24, n. 4.

is rejected by almost all critical authorities.*†

Reverting now to the entries regarding St. James in Martyrologies of the ninth century, we encounter a statement which must at that time have been fresh and startling,—that after his martyrdom in Palestine, his bones were "translated to the furthest limits of Spain, and continued there to be deeply venerated." We thus find how early at Vienne, Paris, and St. Gall, credence was attached to a bold fiction, circulated before A.D. 816, to the effect that the Martyr's bones had been miraculously transported to the North West of Spain, had been there concealed during nearly eight centuries in order that they might escape Saracenic sacrilege, had been then revealed to a hermit or monk named Pelagius, verified by patient scrutiny and in the end solemnly enshrined. The discovery, it appears, had been the subject of an animated correspondence between the King, Alfonso el Casto, the Emperor Charlemagne, and the Pope, Leo III.‡

This fiction, which secured a new lease of life for the Spanish legend, and a vast influence for the cult of the Patron Saint, soon threw the earlier tradition into the shade. Hence, in two of the Martyrologies above cited, the translation is reported but the previous visit is not mentioned. Hence too Cæsarius Archbishop of Tarragona, about A.D. 962 or 984, wrote in defence of the alleged preaching of St. James in Spain against some who only admitted the advent of his remains;

---

* See, besides the Commentators on this passage, the authors referred to by Wiltsch, Geography of the Church, vol. I., p. 18, n. 10.

† Notes, Note 14.

‡ *The Epistola ad Hispanos*, attributed to Leo III., (e.g. by Ledwich) must from internal evidence be considered spurious. It has found no place among the letters of either Charlemagne or Leo, in Migne's *Patrol. Latina*.

and Archbishop Ximenes, in A.D. 1215, while upholding the interest of his own See at Toledo against that of Compostella, again ventured to represent the Apostle's visit as unhistorical. Both of the stories however, as they fit easily into each other, were fused in one narrative, which continued to be repeated, with enlargements and embellishments, not only in the Office Books and the Chronicles of Spain, but also by numerous mediæval writers, was certified by Pope Calixtus II., about A.D. 1120, and was duly incorporated in the *Legenda Aurea* and the *Breviarium Romanum;* though it was destined to be subsequently oppugned by learned polemics like Launoy and Sirmond, and discreetly set aside even by writers so sturdily orthodox as Baronius, the Bollandists, and Tillemont.

The final result of the manipulation through which both parts of the narrative passed may be presented in the following summary. Shortly after the Ascension, about A.D. 34, and therefore not only long before St. Paul projected a journey to Spain, but some time before his conversion, a visit to that country was paid by St. James, the elder son of Zabdiah the fisherman of Gennesareth, whom Spanish writers as well as Dante were fond of designating "el Barone." Though not very successful in his mission the Apostle was in the course of it cheered by a vision of the Virgin, whether in the spirit or in the flesh, seated upon a pillar of jasper or marble, around which he erected the oldest of all churches that have been dedicated to her honour. He was of course obliged to return to Palestine where, as is recorded in the Canonical Acts of the Apostles, he was beheaded about A.D. 44. Immediately afterwards, his body—with or without the head—is averred by our legendaries to have been by divine direction conveyed from Joppa, whether in a mere trough of wood or of stone, or in a scantily manned craft, over the Mediterranean Sea to his former landing-place at Iria Flavia, subsequently called after him "El Padron," and thence to the adjacent town Liberum Donum—the future Compostella. There during nearly eight centuries it remained, hidden in a cavern within a stone sarcophagus which had spontaneously hollowed itself out and closed around it. Having been at last brought to light through an angelic revelation, it was magnificently enshrined. Santiago was thus recognised—how justly he subsequently proved in many a time of need—as the Cynosure of chivalry as well as of patriotic devotion, the Tutelar of the Spanish nation, of its royal line, and of its highest orders of knighthood; and Compostella, during the ages of faith, vied with Rome itself in attracting crowds of pilgrims from far and near, for whom the scallop shell gathered upon the Biscayan beach was a badge as honorific as the palm branch brought from the Holy Land.

The triumphal development which we thus find to have been accorded to one of the two notices that assigned to the Westernmost provinces a share in the Apostolic Sortition presents a remarkable contrast to the neglect and obscurity into which the other notice was destined to fall. It might have been anticipated that the course assigned to Philip and his cult would continue to run parallel to that which was sketched in the legends about James;—and we actually find a statement that the Franks, after their settlement in Gaul as well as while they were still in Sicambria, persisted in regarding Philip as their primal Doctor and Apostle. For this statement, occurring in the Chronicle of Croyland Abbey, which professes to come from Ingulf of the eleventh century, though in its present shape it cannot be older than the fourteenth, one would like to know who are the Frankish authorities (*Hierochronographi*) appealed to by the author.*

---

* The passage is cited by Ussher, *De Brit. Eccles. Primordiis.* Dublinii, 1639. c. XV., p. 652.

MEDIÆVAL LEGENDS

It may commemorate a traditional tendency which really operated among both Franks and Gallo-Romans under the earlier successors of Clovis, but it does not harmonise with what is known regarding the cult which was favoured by Dagobert I., and which became more and more prevalent under the later Merovingian Kings, their Mayors of the Palace, and under the Carolingian Emperors. The two concomitants previously described as requisite to a National recognition of a Patron Saint are found to have been absent in the case of Philip: on the other hand both were united in favour of not a few rivals who attained a diocesan or provincial celebrity, and for whom a National primacy was ultimately claimed. Two of these threw Philip into the shade and distanced all their competitors. The one was believed to have been—not indeed a member of the Apostolic College,—but Isapostolic and invested with a mysterious sanctity; while to the other, though dignified in rank and character, was attached a personal history of a comparatively tame and unromantic caste. Yet it was for the more commonplace Missionary that a permanent ascendancy in the national kalender was brought about; while his rival, although inspiring a deeper awe and a more fervent enthusiasm, had to be satisfied with a widespread, but still only provincial homage.

In elucidating this unexpected result, we shall be occupied for a further space with the medley of traditions and fables which concern the evangelization of Gaul Northern and Southern, but we shall then be able to pass with greater confidence to the accounts of the evangelization of South Western Britain, as we find them handed down in legend and romance.

Section II

Legends about Dionysius among the Franks and the Bethanian Family among the Provençals.

We shall begin with a reference to one method which, as various writers have pointed out, was adopted on behalf of not a few communities in Western Europe, with the view of satisfying their aspirations to trace back the conversion of their ancestors to the primitive days of Christianity,—a method which was satisfied with a less lofty ideal than the renown of discipleship to apostolic visitants like Peter and Paul, James and Philip, but which, in compensation for this self denial, found its way more readily to popular acceptance by associating itself with an element which was, or was believed to be, historical. Some persons were singled out whom tradition or record signalised as the earliest Diocesans, and their dates being pushed back from the second, third, or fourth century to the first, they were identified with companions and delegates of the Apostles. This process was of course much facilitated wherever namesakes of such persons were to be found in the Acts of the Apostles, or in the Pauline Epistles, but it was resorted to likewise even where such aid was lacking. The natural result, especially in districts where no memorials of apostolic visitants had been preserved, was that their very names faded out of popular legend, while those of the recognised founders of the several Sees became more and more prominent.

Examples of this mode of treatment, applied to early occupants of Cisalpine Sees, may be found by a scrutiny of the long list of prelates alleged to have been consecrated in numerous cities of Italy and Sicily by St. Peter, or St. Paul, or by one of the proximate Bishops of Rome, such as Linus and Clemens, or, in a few instances, by Barnabas the legate of St. Paul in Milan, or by Mark the companion of St. Peter in Aquileia. Other examples are recognisable among the early Spanish Ecclesiastics who are reported to have been instructed and ordained by St. James, to have afterwards repaired to Rome for consecration, and to have returned to prosecute their work in the Western Peninsula. The successive steps of the same process are most clearly traceable in Gaul, where many Martyrs, Confessors, and Pastors, who in the oldest extant documents occupy historic ground in the third or fourth centuries, appear in later tradition as holding their commissions direct from St. Paul, St, Peter, or Clement, more frequently than from the isolated Apostle Philip. Of course after the belief that both St. Paul and St. Peter taught and suffered in Rome had come to be generally received, their supremacy could not be affected by whatever homage might be accorded to the patron-saints of any Italian province; while the happy device adopted in the ninth century, which united the original legend of St. James with its marvellous sequel, obviated any chance that the lustre of his name might be dimmed by lesser luminaries in Bracara or Seville, no matter at what period they were supposed to have reached their zenith. In regard to Gaul, including Cisrhenane Germany, we find echoes of a rumour or a surmise, that it was traversed by St. Paul, St. Peter, and Clement (not to say by St. James likewise), as well as by Philip, and that numerous stations were left by them in charge of missionaries or proselytes whom they had prepared for pastoral work. But it was never whispered that those Apostles had themselves remained in the country, or that their relics had been brought back to it, and it was not with their names but with those of their reputed successors that religious foundations of local celebrity were associated. Hence their memory was never drawn out from the twilight of hagiological theory, while the fame of succeeding teachers was embalmed in traditions or myths of an enduring and expansive character.

Among the personages who came to be antedated and transformed in the way here described, no place could be found for the most distinguished ornaments of the early Gallican Church, such as Martin of Tours, Remigius of Rheims, or Hilarius of Poitiers, because their historic places and associations were too well defined and too generally known to admit of their being shunted to a remote epoch, or treated as semi-mythical. In regard to the Alexandrine Pothinus and the Smyrniote Irenæus, by whose teaching Lyons and Vienne had been really ennobled in the second century, no temptation was felt to tamper with their authentic memorials by introducing any hollow and baseless assumptions. But the tendency which had once set in found ample scope in dealing with others. Gregory of Tours, about A.D. 590, has noticed each of those eminent pastors in his proper place, and he has also had occasion to mention seven missionaries sent into Gaul by Pope Fabianus in or about A.D. 250; viz: two Martyrs, Saturninus of Toulouse and Dionysius of Paris, and five Confessors, G[r]atianus of Tours, Trophimus of Arles, Paulus of Narbonne, Stremonius of Auvergne, Martialis of Limoges.* This notice entirely ignores various pretensions concerning those pastors which seem to have been set up about Gregory's time, or perhaps in some cases much earlier. In the preceding century while Arles—of old, a great Roman Mart, afterwards the capital of the Burgundian Kingdom, and of Septimania—was successfully vieing with Vienne for the dignity of a provincial metropolis, and even competing with Trèves—that *altera Roma* or chief seat of empire in North-

---

* See Greg. Turon, *Historia Francorum*, Lib. I., c.c. 27, 28, 35, 36, ap. Migne, *Patrol. Lat.* t. lxxi., coll. 174-5, 179, 180.

MEDIÆVAL LEGENDS

western Europe—for primatial jurisdiction over Gaul, it was urged upon the pontiffs Zosimus and Leo I. (about A.D. 417 and 450), and is said to have been admitted by them, that S. Trophimus had been sent from Rome into Gaul by the Apostles,—specially by St. Peter. Again, the contemporary of Gregory of Tours, Venantius Fortunatus, who appears to have resided in Gaul during the last quarter of the sixth century, and to have died about A.D. 609, while Bishop of Poitiers, relates in his rhetorical strain that, after the Ascension, missionary bishops were ordained "by the Apostles," instancing Saturninus of Toulouse, Felix and Paulus of Narbonne; and further he states that Dionysius, commissioned "by the successors of the Apostles," proceeded to Paris, which became his See, and that there he was martyred, along with his Presbyter Rusticus, and Eleutherius his Archdeacon.

The same Dionysius, as is well known, was looked up to with veneration by the descendants of Clovis. By Dagobert I., and all the following Kings, he was regarded as their especial patron; and the Monastery built in his honour by Chlotaire I., continued from first to last to enjoy immunities and benefactions conferred by them, and their Mayors of the Palace. Now in most of the extant charters of this Monastery the saint is described, with all his miraculous gifts, as simply the founder of the See, who suffered martyrdom along with his Presbyter and Archdeacon; but in one, which, genuine or not, professes to have been issued by Thierry or Theodoric IV., he and his co-martyrs are said to have been sent "in the earliest post-apostolic age, specially ordained by St. Clement, successor to Peter the Apostle."

As we have remarked already in this chapter, when a coincidence in names was observed between the supposed catechumens of the Apostles and persons mentioned in the New Testament, the circumstance was often turned to good

THE HOLY GRAIL

account, and this we find well exemplified in the identification of the missionaries to Arles, Narbonne, and Paris, with three of St. Paul's friends, Trophimus (Acts xx., 4), Sergius Paulus (Acts xiii., 7), and Dionysius the Areopagite (Acts xvii., 34).

Let us glance at the case of the Parisian Martyr, which, by cool and careful criticism working on good materials, has been presented in a light exceptionally clear. It appears that in several monastic biographies written during the reign of Charlemagne, and in the Acts of a Synod held at Paris, A.D. 824, not only was the statement repeated that Dionysius had been sent into Gaul by Clement, and had suffered death under Domitian, but it was suggested that he was no other than the Areopagite. This notion was confirmed by Hincmar, Archbishop of Rheims, in a letter addressed to Louis the Pious ("le Debonaire"), A.D. 823, and it was elaborately set forth in 834, by Hilduin, Abbot of St. Denis, under the auspices of Charles the Bald. It became dominant among the Franks through the advocacy of the illustrious Johannes Scotus (Erigena), who, about 859, revised and completed a translation of the theosophic books which passed under the name of the famous Athenian Senator, and which, in that age and long after, were extravagantly appreciated in Western Europe. Elsewhere too this idea attracted influential adherents. Thus Methodius, Patriarch of Constantinople, and his translator the Roman Abbot Anastasius Sinaita, substituted this Gallican invention for what had been the constant Greek tradition (traced up to Aristides of the second century), that the Areopagite died and was buried in Athens, where he had been appointed Bishop by St. Paul. Out of a mere theory soon emerged a story—consistent in its outline, though vacillating in regard to dates and details—to the effect that this most gifted convert of St. Paul, after the Apostle was put to death by Nero, left his Athenian See and repaired to Rome, whence he was despatched by Clement to Gaul, that having landed near the mouths of the Rhone, he and twelve companions travelled northward to the valley of the Seine, and that, at the close of a long and successful pastorate, he and his Archpresbyter and Archdeacon heroically met their doom, about A.D. 100, on the height previously named "*Mont Mercre*" (*Mons Mercurii*), but thenceforth "*Mont Martre*" (*Mons Martyrum*). The very first elements of this legend, however, were ignored in the ninth century by Usuard in Paris and Ado in Vienne, as well as by Rabanus Maurus and Walafrid Strabo beyond the Rhine. Letaldus of St. Mesmin (near Orleans), so late as A.D. 980, was led by his historic sense to return to the statement of Gregory of Tours,* and even in the twelfth century Abélard may not have had a monopoly of scepticism, though the audacious expression which he gave to it, within the very precincts of St. Denis, caused his ignominious expulsion.

Hagiolatry has usually been as easy-going—as well disposed to give and take—as polytheism itself. The exaltation of the Parisian Tutelar was not likely to awaken jealousy, nor, therefore, to encounter serious opposition, when reported in other Dioceses which were ambitious of elevating their respective founders in a similar way. Rival pretensions were amicably and spontaneously adjusted wherever the local evangelists were represented as having come into Gaul in company with Dionysius, whether as equals or as subordinates. Such a compromise was exemplified in the case of Julianus of Le Mans, Sanctinus of Verdun, Mansuetus of Toul and numerous others, but was rudely disturbed in Limousin during a great part of the eleventh century, by a strange burst of fanaticism, which asserted for Martialis a unique preeminence—a parity with Barnabas, with Paul, with the original Twelve Apostles.

---

* See *Vita S. Juliani*, ap. Migne, *Patrologia Latina*, t. cxxxvii., p. 782.

THE HOLY GRAIL

Outside of the Frankish pale, in districts which had long borne the stamp of Roman civilisation—military, civil, and religious,—the vaunts of what was deemed an upstart capital met with but scant deference. Thus Trèves, Cologne, and Tongres adhered loyally to their traditionary cult of Valerius, Eucharius (or Eucharis) and Maternus, each of whom was alleged to have been a disciple of S. Peter or of his successor, while the last of the three was also identified in some quarters with the son of the widow of Nain (Luke vii., 11-15). A similar instinct continued to guide the historic cities of Burgundy, Provence, and Aquitaine. It was due to the slow operation of political causes, chiefly the success of the house of Capet in gradually annexing, by finesse or force, adjacent provinces to their dominion, that Paris at last became the centre and cynosure of France; and it was an outcome of the same protracted process that the fame of Denis of Mont-Joye, identified with Dionysius of the Areopagus, overshadowed that of saints who had passed for his co-evals and co-equals.

The coincidence of a patron's name, whether Greek or Roman, with one honourably mentioned in the New Testament—of which Hilduin, Hincmar, and their allies took a fair advantage—was one that could be appealed to in many localities, and most readily in the Southern Provinces, where Greek names of persons as well as places, memorials of the ancient Phocaean colonization, were interspersed in the prevailing Roman nomenclature. We have already seen that Paul of Narbonne was surmised to have been the same with Sergius Paulus, the official who attached himself to his namesake the Apostle in Cyprus (Acts xiii, 7), and that Trophimus of Arles was identified with the Ephesian Trophimus who accompanied Paul in his missionary journeys, and in regard to whose subsequent history Graeco-Roman traditions were divergent. An expedient resorted to by partisans of Arles was

MEDIÆVAL LEGENDS

not likely to be overlooked by those who upheld the prestige of Vienne. So Crescens, an early occupant of the latter See, was given out by Archbishop Ado, for instance, as that Crescens whose visit to Galatia (mentioned in 2 Tim., IV., 10), was, as has been already noticed, misinterpreted at an early period (cp. Eusebius H. E. III., 4), as directed towards Gallia. Similar guesses, which, however, the evidences adduced do not enable us to trace back to the same period with those already noticed, were brought into play regarding some other Bishops, such as Clement of Metz, Rufus of Avignon (or Pau), Cornelius of Vannes in distant Bretagne, identified respectively with the Philippian Clement (Phil. IV., 3), with Rufus, who is mentioned in Paul's Epistle to the Romans (XVI., 23), and who was perhaps the son of Simon of Cyrene noticed in the Gospel of Mark (XV. 21), and with Cornelius the Centurion in Caeserea (Acts X., 1). Regarding Parmenas,—one of the seven original Deacons, named in Acts VI., 5, whose martyrdom at Philippi, affirmed by Greek tradition, which includes him with Clemens and Rufus, is admitted by Archbishop Ado,—he is alleged in a legendary work, already referred to as perhaps belonging to the ninth century, to have come into Gaul in a missionary expedition organised by S.S. Peter and Paul, to have become Bishop in Avignon, and to have there attained the martyr's crown. Along with him and Trophimus of Arles are enumerated the Corinthian Sosthenes (mentioned in Acts XVIII., 17, and 1 Cor., I., 1.), and the Philippian Epaphras or Epaphroditus (mentioned in Phil. II., 25), along with the two women Euodia and Syntyche whom Paul commended to Epaphras' care (Phil. IV., 2, 3). Both the men are treated as subordinates of Trophimus and as simple evangelists or itinerant preachers, and Epaphras and Syntyche are said to have returned to the East, a statement not extended to Sosthenes and Euodia.

THE HOLY GRAIL

The Legend in which these names appear treats of a very early expedition despatched under Apostolic auspices to Provence. In that district it appears to have originated and grown up under various modifications. Both there and elsewhere it awakened extraordinary interest, by not only classing the conductors of the enterprise in vague terms among the seventy disciples of our Lord, but even specifying persons, more or fewer in its different versions, who are recorded in the Gospels as having received from Him special blessings, or as having been united with Him in the closest ties of hospitality and affection. All the versions recognised in the central figures Mary and Martha of Bethany, and most of them exhibit Lazarus also as the prime mover and director.

But the presence of Lazarus in the expedition is explicitly negatived in one version, which, though not the oldest or simplest in conception, is important because it is the most elaborate in method and execution. It is in some of its MSS. daringly ascribed to Rabanus Maurus of Fulda, and it may not improbably have been composed by some one resident in, or connected with, Provence in the ninth or the tenth century. It is, as its title bears, a biography of the two sisters, appealing to various older lives of S. Mary Magdalene as its sources, and is itself followed in various other lives of the same saint. We have still extant a number of these lives, a few of which may present specimens or contain fragments of the earlier class; but most, even when written in Latin, appear to be derivatives. Now, as has just been stated, the life attributed to Rabanus Maurus, discarding the agency of Lazarus, substituted for him, as leaders of the missionary band, two persons whose names have been associated with Episcopal Sees in cities contiguous to the place of landing. Starting from the traditional postulate of the partition of the world into apostolic provinces, this narrative represents SS.

MEDIÆVAL LEGENDS

Peter and Paul, to whom Western Europe was allotted, as delegating seventeen of their own or their Master's disciples for the Dioceses of Gaul, and seven others for those of Spain,—the array of their names agreeing in the main with that which is found elsewhere in analogous lists. It then narrows its scope to the vicinity of the Rhone below Vienne. The Viennese See itself with its founder, Crescens, it passes unnoticed, but it signalises two bishops in the Viennese territory, viz., Parmenas (not Rufus) in Avignon, and Eupropius in Orange, as also the inevitable Trophimus in Arles, and a hitherto unknown Maximinus in the double charge of Aix and Marseilles. It is within the Dioceses of Maximinus and Parmenas that the two sisters from Bethany are described as passing the thirty years of their residence in Provence. Moreover Maximinus is recognised as chief of the voyagers, with the titles *Pontifex* and *Archipraesul*, while Parmenas appears as his lieutenant, and is designated *Archidiaconus* rather than *Archipresbyter*, in allusion seemingly to his name being inscribed among the seven deacons, after the protomartyr Stephen, and the evangelist Philip. How men thus distinguished were not provided with more famous names than one which is found in but a single text of Scripture, and one which is not Scriptural at all, may be most easily explained on the assumption that both names were borrowed from diocesan rolls which supplied none more suitable. This assumption appears to be safe as regards Maximinus, a familiar Latin family name borne by ecclesiastics in various parts of Gaul, and perpetuated by the township of St. Maximin near Aix, which grew up around a priory, as that grew out of the oratory of the founder.

Be that as it may, it is recorded further that, in pursuance of an arrangement suggested by the sisters before they left the shores of Palestine, the leader, Maximinus, acted during the voyage as especial guardian and representative of Mary,

THE HOLY GRAIL

while his lieutenant stood in the same relation to Martha and her handmaid Marcella. Thus the association in each case was not merely prelusive of the bond that was to be formed between the chief pastors and the ordinary members of two settled communities, but was of a closer character, an outcome of affectionate trust. The legend, however, does not hint at troth-plighting, or any similar tie. Indeed no such idea could have commended itself to monastic writers, who generally advocated the celibacy of the clergy, secular as well as regular, and lauded virginity as the very queen of virtues,—angelic indeed, but essential to human perfection. This besides accorded best with the types of character always assigned in Western legends to the Tutelary Sisters. Martha, the opulent and liberal *Hospita Christi, Albergatrice di Christo*, the mistress of the house upon the Mount of Olives, so assiduous in attendance on her Divine Guest—she needed no other assistant than her handmaid (*pedisequa*) whom she had brought with her, while true to her distinctive character *La Travailleuse*, she passed from hamlet to hamlet working miracles of charity and mercy, which culminated when at Tarrascon she encountered and slew the fell dragon, under whose ravages the population was dwindling away.

Mary, again, was conceived in most forms of this legend, as, indeed, in Mediaeval legends generally, as the Bethanian and the Magdalene both in one; the sojourner beneath the family roof in Bethany and the lady of a manor at Magdala, on the Lake of Galilee; the penitent who was rescued from demoniac possession; the absorbed listener to the words spoken "as never man spake;" the perfume-shedder in the house of Simon; the first to whom her risen Lord was revealed. It is recorded that she was one of the privileged spectators of the Assumption, and was spontaneously greeted by all present as inheritrix of the honours then vacated,—second only

MEDIÆVAL LEGENDS

to the cult of the Virgin Mother,—which she afterwards received throughout Latin Christendom. After her landing at Marseilles she was believed to have passed the latter half of her life, as an hermit and ascetic, in the waste land contiguous to Aix, still called *La Sainte Beaume,* from the cavern cell which was her abode, and which was afterwards trodden by many a pilgrim foot. Our authorities assure us that when the euthanasia of the Magdalene arrived, Maximinus performed the last rite at the tomb which he had prepared for her, within the Abbey which bore his name, and that, when on the eighth day after, the spirit of Martha also passed away, her interment took place under supernatural agency, in presence of Parmenas and other friends, within a chapel which she had herself erected at Tarrascon. It is further noticed that Marcella, to whom has been ascribed a biography of her mistress, considering her mission to be then completed, returned to Palestine. The place of the subsequent martyrdom of Parmenas is not precisely stated. The sepulchre of Maximinus is described as close to that of the patroness, of whose fame his own was but a feeble reflex.

As for other versions of the legend, it has been already stated that, being cruder in conception and less guarded against criticism, they seem to present an older type; but the documents in which they are preserved are of very dubious date and questionable authorship, being chiefly Lives of Saints and local Office Books, which have been referred at random to any age between the fifth century and the eleventh. Among the best known and most authoritative works in which such versions were subsequently incorporated, it will suffice to specify the *Legenda Aurea* and the *Breviarium Romanum.**

---

* See *Legenda Aurea,* cap. xcvi., pp. 409-415, cap. cv., pp. 444-7; Breviarium Romanum, *S. Marthae Vita, Julii* 29 and *Julii* 25; Fail-

THE HOLY GRAIL

They do not all concur with the version already described in assigning the expedition of which they treat to the fourteenth year after the Ascension (A.D. 47 or 48), since some of them carry it back to the first year after that event (A.D. 34, or to some intermediate period; nor do they all regard it as fitted out in pursuance of the Apostolic Sortition, and bringing in a body the numerous diocesans among whom Gaul was to be parcelled out. Some of them, indeed, substitute for Parmenas a person hitherto unnoticed, who has been arbitrarily identified with the youth born blind, on whom our Lord conferred the sense of sight (John ix.), and whose name Chelidonius (corrupted in some copies into Cedonius and even Sydonius) has the ring of the old Ionian minstrelsy, and may have been an heirloom from the old Ionian colony. When both these persons are included they, with Maximinus, form a clerical triad, (analogous to that of the Parisian legend, composed of Dionysius, Rusticus and Eleutherius), and while Maximinus is styled Archipraesul, and Parmenas Archidiaconus, the new comer Chelidonius, is interposed as Archipresbyter. They are all at one in affirming the presence of Lazarus, who takes charge of his sisters and conducts the expedition, though he, as a soldier or knight, is treated as deferring to Maximinus in the exercise of his priestly functions. In some copies he and his fellow voyagers, comprising not a few of the seventy disciples of our Lord, figure not as free agents, but as thrust out by the enemies of the faith in a lugger unprovided with sails or oars. But under whatever auspices he left Palestine, we are assured that Lazarus arrived safe in Marseilles, and there exchanged the sword for the crosier, being consecrated by his friend Maximinus, who for his part took the charge of Aix. One vera-

---

lon, *Monuments Inédits sur L'Apostolat de Sainte Marie Madeleine en Provence, &c.* 2 vols., 4to., Paris, 1848.

cious document—the *Acta* which are unblushingly attributed to Alexander of Brescia in the first century—records a visit paid by that prelate to both,—to Lazarus at Marseilles as well as to Maximinus at Aix. And there long hovered a tradition around the abbey of St. Sauveur in Marseilles that the crypt over which it was built had been the vaulted prison in which Lazarus awaited his martyrdom.*

From the preceding epitome it appears that the legend of Lazarus—broadly contrasted with those relating to Dionysius, Trophimus, and other pupils of SS. Peter and Paul—presents traits which strikingly remind us of the marvels told about Joseph of Arimathaea, and James, the eldest son of Zebedee. It might well seem that those who moulded it, residing within or nigh to Marseilles, and anxious to maintain the renown of their time-honoured city, could not brook that distant and obscure ports on the Atlantic should have a monopoly of credit for sheltering the first Christian missionaries who had crossed the Mediterranean from the shores of Palestine, and that, in a spirit of emulation, they sought so to construct

---

* Various metrical pieces concerning Mary Magdalene and her relatives in Provence have been edited in recent times; one in Provençal, printed by Bory, Marseille, 1862; one in early French by Guillaume le Clere, printed by P. Reinsch, in Herrig's Archiv für das Studium der Neueren Sprachen und Literatur. Bd. LXIV. Heft 1, pp. 87-94; and one in early English, given in two forms by C. Horstmann, *Sammlung Altenglischer Legenden*, Heilbronn, 1878, pp. 148-170. A rare tract entitled "La Vie de Maria Magdalena, contenant plusieurs miracles, comment elle, son Frere le Lazare et Marthe sa Soeur vindrent a Marseille, et comment elle convertit le Duc et la Duchesse, &c.," printed at Lyon, by Pierre de la Haye, 1605, (composed perhaps about 1500), is referred to by Ideler, *Geschichte der Alt-Französischen Literatur*, p. 236, and by Le Comte de Douchet, *Dictionnaire des Legendes du Christianisme*.

their narrative that its protagonist should, in his rank, his associations and his adventures, approximate the fame of the Apostle of Spain himself.

Another remarkable analogy between the two legends would come into relief if we should go on to review a series of translations and re-appearances which, according to the Provençal narratives, the mortal remains of Lazarus and his sisters were destined to experience. But to recite that sequel of the Massilian legend is not requisite for the object which we have been seeking to attain, viz., for the elucidation, by means of analogous and kindred legends, of the missionary voyaging and adventures of Joseph, the Arimathaean, to which we are now ready to proceed. A succinct notice of that sequel therefore is relegated to an appendix, which only those readers who may take sufficient interest in the subject are invited to peruse, while others will pass on at once to the ensuing chapter.

CHAPTER VII.

Glastonbury and its Traditions of Joseph of Arimathaea, of St. Patrick, and of other Saintly Visitors.

ALL extant accounts of the operations of Joseph of Arimathaea, extrinsic and subsequent to the close of his record in the Gospels, have been previously shown to range themselves under two classes; the one comprehending those which recognised the old legend that his imprisonment after the sepulture of Christ was prolonged during forty or forty-two years; the other including those which either ignored his imprisonment or made it of very short duration. Since, according to the former view he was, during his long seclusion, enlightened as well as sustained through divine communion, he would be found at the close fully qualified to take an independent and conspicuous part in the dissemination of the new faith; but according to the other view, he was conceived to have placed himself under the direction of the Apostle Philip,—who, in concert with St. John and St. James the Less, was the principal organiser of foreign missions,— to have accompanied that Apostle, about A.D., 44, or as late as A.D., 63, to Gaul, and to have been thence despatched to initiate the evangelisation of Britain.

This is the place to notice—if it be needful to notice it at all—that one account associated Joseph in his voyage to Gaul, not with Philip of Bethsaida, but with that more famous Evangelist of Provence, Lazarus of Bethany. Of course reasons might readily suggest themselves which would seem to favour the latter association. Joseph and Lazarus were understood, even if they had not been long acquainted with each other, to be assimilated in their habits and sympathies as knights or soldiers (*milites*), and as holders of neighbouring estates. They were now united in the same cause, and they were alike obnoxious to the Jewish Rulers, the one because of the miracle which had restored him to life, the other because of the honour he had shown to the Messiah whom they had despised and rejected. And if, while the one had been avowedly a disciple and bosom friend of Jesus, the other had for a time watched passing events from a distance, and maintained some reserve in the expression of his convictions, the more suitable might it seem that when all hesitation was finally abandoned, the neophite should seek to receive instruction from one who had been so intimately associated with their Divine Master.

It is, however, needless to assign reasons for a variation of the legend which has only attracted attention through the prominence given to it by Cardinal Baronius, and which has not been traced further back than to the *Chronikon* of Pseudo-Dexter, from whose capricious fancy it appears to have originated. That writer has nowhere treated expressly of St. Philip's presence in Western Europe, and so has had no occasion to specify any of his coadjutors there; but he has distinctly rehearsed the Massilian legend about Lazarus and his fellow-voyagers, and finding among the names catalogued by his authorities two, Parmenas and Chelidonius, which did not appear to him sufficiently noteworthy, he deemed it a good stroke to substitute for them that of the Arimathaean, as much better known, and capable of being turned to better account. His so-called continuator Helecas has followed him in replacing Parmenas by Joseph, but he has retained the name of Chelidonius (or Cedonius), mentioned in chapter vi. as identified with the youth who was blind from his birth till our Lord met him and conferred on him the sense of sight (John ix.).

MEDIÆVAL LEGENDS

If we now take up the more generally received account that Joseph's leader and companion was the Apostle Philip, we find it recorded four or five centuries before Pseudo-Dexter's fabrication appeared, but we shall be disappointed if we look for its vouchers in that earlier period when the legends of Compostella, or of Marseilles, or even of Paris, obtained currency. We have previously had occasion (chapter iii.) to refer to the latest reports of the evidence regarding the Resurrection and the Ascension, given by Joseph before the Commissioner of Tiberius in Judea—reports embodied in Western compilations constructed between the seventh and eleventh centuries; but between these and the oldest published accounts of his appearance as a missionary in Western Europe there is as already remarked a blank, and the missing links which might bridge it over have not yet been brought to light from any repertory of ecclesiastical or legendary lore. Not till the twelfth century is the old Isidorian tradition of Philip's arrival in Gaul followed up quite suddenly, and without a warning of any novelty, by a statement that Joseph of Arimathaea was his coadjutor there, and thence proceeded under his direction to evangelize Britain. The eminent writer who gave his countenance to this newly-started idea seems to have assumed that the missionaries entered this Island by the Bristol Channel, and as no scheme was known to him, even if one had been already devised, which would imply a locality north of that Channel in Glamorganshire as the scene of their operations, he has felt no hesitation in assigning, as the locality where the work was carried on, a district south of the Channel in North-west Somerset.

As is well known, the Benedictine Abbey of Glastonbury was, from about A.D. 946, when it received an austerer rule from Dunstan, the greatest of its historical Abbots, until its dissolution and spoliation in A.D. 1539, the most venerated

THE HOLY GRAIL

and influential monastic establishment in England. But it had to maintain under the Anjevin Kings a severe struggle for autonomy against the Bishoprick of Wells, and therefore, like other monasteries in similar circumstances, it resorted to the forging of charters and other muniments, and persuaded writers of good repute to uphold its privileges and immunities as derived from the most remote antiquity. So William, the Librarian of Malmesbury who, in his Histories of the Anglian Kings and Anglian Bishops, suggested for his own Wiltshire Monastery a date coeval, and a dignity almost co-equal with that of the Mitred Abbey in Somersetshire, was prevailed on to devote to the latter a copious monograph, in which its unique antiquity and unrivalled preeminence are dilated on with a fond and unquestioning faith. In some copies of his Histories long extracts from this work have been inserted in successive recensions, not by the author himself, but evidently by transcribers anxious to circulate the Glastonbury hypothesis; and since, even in the monograph, William was considered by ardent partisans to have been too chary in the use of the materials supplied to him, there have been foisted into its texture some remarkable statements, of which there is no documentary trace anterior to the Legendaries of the fourteenth and fifteenth centuries. It will be convenient here to advert to some of the points, which in handling his brief the writer has put forward, connecting the case made out for the Abbey with various events and personages of what was popularly accepted as the early history of the South Britons, and then to mark how the accounts so presented were made to lead up to the Arimathaean legend and to modify the course assigned to it.

While the terms in which the erection of a Minster at Glastonbury by Ini, King of Wessex, who reigned from A.D. 688 to 725, is notified in the Anglo Saxon Chronicle, and by

MEDIÆVAL LEGENDS

Florence of Worcester, may suggest that it was only then called into being, there are extant in the letters of St. Boniface, and in the biography of that Saint by Willibald, authentic evidences that a monastic establishment of British origin existed in the district before it was reduced by the West Saxon conquerors about A.D. 682. William knew nothing of the figment hazarded in a contemporary Welsh Chronicle,* which transferred the benefactious of Ini, as well as his other characteristic acts, to an Armorican Prince, Ivor, successor to the last Cadwaladyr, but he on good grounds assumed that the pious munificence of the West Saxon King took shape in enlarging the buildings, and regulating the constitution of a monastery endeared under a rudimentary form to his British subjects. Those subjects, as it is recorded, reoccupied the district of Glastonbury in 683. They continued to watch for any opportunity of regaining their independence, and Ini's anxiety to conciliate them appears from his Code of Laws which provided for the *Wealhcyn,* as well as for the *Angelcyn* within his realm, and which remained in force till the days of Aelfrid. William has indeed relied too confidently upon Charters bearing the signatures of Ini, of sub-kings and prelates his contemporaries, and even of some of his predecessors, including Kenwalk, A.D. 670,—Charters the more remarkable of which prove so much as to prove nothing at all, except their own spuriousness. He has even referred to a British Charter in favor of the Old Church at Iniswitrin issued by an unnamed King† of

---

* In the *Brut-y-Tywysogion* (Myvirian Archæology vol II., p. 470), which used to be wrongly ascribed to Caradoe of Llancarvan, followed by the *Brut Ienan [Jenan?] Brachva* (ibid p. 471); this Ivor is said to have "founded the great Priory in the Isle of Avallon"=Glastonbury, A.D. 683.

† The name is supplied by Dr. Guest (Archæological Journal, vol.

THE HOLY GRAIL

Damnonia (*Dyvnaint*) A.D. 601, and he has cited the names of Abbats ruling between that date and the time of the Conquest, the earlier of which he looked upon as British, succeeded by others of the Saxon type. There is no inherent improbability in such surmises, nor in the supposition that patronage was, from wise policy, extended to the monastery by princes who, after the Christianization of Wessex in 636, lapsed into paganism, or passed and repassed from the one cult to the other. The choice by Ini,—and according to William by his predecessor Cynewealh likewise,—of Brittannic or rather Hyberno-Britannic sanctuaries, such as Glastingaburh and Maeldunesburg, found parallels, within the same century, in the adjacent kingdom of Mercia, as when Bishop Eghorn under Coenred of Mercia built the Church at Eovisham on a spot hallowed by an apparition of the Virgin, and Offa of Mercia reared the stately pile at Verulam in honor of the Romano-Britannic Proto-martyr St. Alban.

When we step back into the fifth and sixth centuries, the stormy period which intervened between the withdrawal of the Roman Legionaries and the high tide of the Teutonic conquest, while the Cymri exhausted all their resources in incessant conflict with Pictish and Scottish marauders from Caledonia and Hibernia, an incident recorded by William affords a curious glimpse into the way in which Glastonbury was affected by the migrations and vicissitudes of the races concerned in the struggle. It is told in relation to a descendant of a Cumbrian or Strath-Clyde potentate, Cunedda Wledig, who with his stalwart sons figures prominently in Welsh records as having expelled from Gwynedd or North Wales cer-

---

XVI., p. 129), as *Gwrgan Varvtrwch*, "with the greatest likelihood," Mr. Freeman remarks; see "Glastonbury British and English," in Macmillan's Magazine, October 1880.

MEDIÆVAL LEGENDS

tain tribes of *Gwyddel*, and especially *Gwyddel Ffichti* (Picts) previously settled in that region. One, perhaps the youngest, of twelve brothers who claimed Cunedda as their ancestor, is said to have been directed to his predestined resting place in Yniswydrin, the marshy district enclosed between the River Brue and its tributary streams, by one of those animal guides which mythology associates with so many city founders,—the analogy in this case being closest to the *Sus Alba* or *scrofa* which indicated to Aeneas the site of the future Alba Longa. Having followed his sow, and found her suckling her brood beneath an apple tree which stood solitary in the then humid waste, adjacent to an old and ruined church, he there took up his abode, and thence forward even to William's days tradition still spoke of the *ealdecirce suge* or "old church sow" and the *ealdcyrcenes apple* or "apples of the old church." Two new designations are said to have thus accrued to the district, one of every day use, employed by prose writers Saxon and Norman, as also in some Welsh documents, the other preferred in the diction of poetry and romance professedly of British origin. From the name of Cunedda's descendant, which in William's text appears as "Glasteing," but which must have been rather Glasti or Glaste (an heirloom from primeval times meaning "Woad-stained"), was derived *Glasteia=Glast-ey*, "Glaste's Isle," or *Glastonia* "Glaste's Town or Stead," or *Glastinga-byrig* "the Hold of Glaste's Family or Clan." On the other hand we find also the more euphonious *Insula Avallonia* or *Avalonia,* and this William has deduced from the British *Aval*=apple and apple-tree. Having given this etymon he discreetly stops; the remark which he might have added that "Avallon" exactly represents the Welsh *avallen*=apple-yard or orchard would not have suited so well the legend which he transmits. He probably reflected also that a term equivalent to "orchard" could not have been applied distinctively to a boggy district, which by the hypothesis was but partially if at all reclaimed, though long afterwards it might perhaps, even in the cider districts of the South West, have denoted the vicinity of the great Abbey, if the inmates had lavished there that horticultural skill and industry which were conspicuous around so many establishments of the Benedictine Order. Be that as it may, it is well to note here (reserving fuller discussion for another place) that William's treatise is perhaps the earliest document in which the two topographical terms are clearly used as synonimous. In the Life and Letters of St. Boniface already cited, [page 73], composed before A.D. 700, the prosaic term Glastingabury is used, and in a Life of St. Dunstan, written in the tenth century, the name is Glastonia. In a Life of Gildas ascribed to Caradoc of Llancarvan, in the twelfth century the name is again Glastonia; but in the *Brut y Tywysogion*, composed after 1282, probably by some other British Chronicler, as well as in the epitome of it, the *Brut Ienan Brachva*, occurs the substituted *Ynys Avallon*. In later documents inspired from Glastonbury, and in such wild compositions as the Triads, Avallon or Avalonia continues to be the favourite designation.

The passage in the life of Gildas just referred to notices benefits conferred on the monastery by the far-famed Arthur, but this is evidently independent of the statements regarding that patriot chieftain made by Geoffry of Monmouth, and by our Monk of Malmesbury. The former, in the first half of the twelfth century, has related how his hero was conveyed from the fatal field of Camlan to be cured, if it were possible, of his deadly wounds in the *Insula Avalonia*, the locality of which he has refrained from indicating; but his contemporary William, or else an interpolator—followed by Gerald Barry and others—states that the *Insula Avalonia*, the identity of which with Glastonia he assumes as undoubted, was the retreat in which Arthur ended his life, and that there he

MEDIÆVAL LEGENDS

was buried. Though in the History of the Anglian Kings the tomb of Arthur is declared to be nowhere recognised, yet in a curious section found in various copies of "The Antiquities of Glastonbury"—a section expressly devoted to this subject—minute details are given by way of determining the exact position of his grave along with that of Guinevere, his Queen, and an epitaph is adduced, in all the variant forms of which the *Insula Avalonia* is unfailingly recorded as the royal resting-place.

While lists of princely benefactors—traced even further back than to Arthur in the British annals, including also both the Saxon and the Danish sovereigns, and terminating with the Plantagenets—illustrate the position, the claims, and the fortunes of the Glastonian community, its interior life and organisation are more distinctly revealed in casual sketches, half historic, half legendary, of early Saints whom it registered among its visitors or inmates as having administered, or modified, or constructed its discipline. In such sketches there constantly recurs a well-marked trait, contrasting the hagiography of the Western, and especially the British Kelts with the ordinary tenor of their traditions, in a state of society which Christian influences were permeating but fitfully and slowly. While not only alien peoples but kindred septs were divided by chronic jealousies, and engaged in frequent warfare,—even their truces leading to fresh ruptures, their leagues to internecine conflicts, their hospitable feastings to scenes of carnage—the heralds or the Gospel appear in these troubled times, if not always as successful peacemakers, yet at least as personally animated by a catholic spirit, exempt from any prejudices of race or party in the prosecution of their work, and no more deterred by differences of nationality, or even of language, than by the physical difficulties and privations with which they had to struggle. Ever in quest of the new and the marvellous, lovers of change, adventure, and strenuous action, aspiring through their communion with Nature to communion with Nature's God; eager to interchange religious ideas and experiences with brethren in the Faith, as well as to diffuse the light of truth over regions still dark and desolate; those untiring pioneers and unconscious Freemasons appear in their legends forever on the move, toiling over pathless wolds and wafted in slight coracles over stormy seas, from hermitage to hermitage, from convent to convent, while they either attract proselytes to new stations or enter into brotherhoods already established, now as students, now as instructors. Britons, Armoricans and Hibernians, Kymrians and Lloegrians, Picts and Scots, the wanderers could count everywhere upon a loyal and genial welcome, unless they should fall in with bands of pagan marauders from the German Ocean.

To writers familar with such representations, as the Glastonian traditionists and their Malmesbury ally could not fail to be, the journeyings and achievements which they had to recount concerning eminent saints, whom fame associated with the great Abbey, must have seemed to be quite in keeping with the ordinary course of history. Prominent among these, as sketched in the treatise of William of Malmesbury, are the Cumbrian Gildas of Strathclyde, the Kymrian Dewi ("The Waterman") or David, and Patrick, the evangelist of Ireland. It appeared to our author perfectly natural, and so he has faithfully recorded that the destined Tutelar of Wales made a pilgrimage to Jerusalem, and there received from the Patriarch a miraculous altar; that on his return having brought with him that precious boon, or had it sent after him, he reposited it in the old church of St. Mary in Yniswidrin, where it acquired the designation of "The Sapphire," from the rarest of the treasures piled upon it, a stone understood to be a sapphire of unusual size and lustre. Further, the story ran that he built and dedicated to St. Mary a new church, closely adjacent to the old one, and that he did this because, when about to impart episcopal consecration to the old church, he had been prohibited by a vision of our Lord, who announced that He had Himself ages ago consecrated it to His mother. This story William had no hesitation in transmitting, and indeed it was not felt to savour of irreverence, when analogous fabrications passed current regarding the sanctuaries at Evesham and Westminster, and at Einsiedeln in Canton Schwytz. In regard to the unquiet life of Gildas, the Wise and the Querulous, William has not stopped to transcribe the most notable incidents recorded elsewhere. For instance, he has not mentioned that that stern denouncer of sins and defections in high places transferred his labours for a while from Britain to Ireland, and thence bore away a wondrous Bell, which he conveyed to Rome, but brought thence to Wales, and bestowed upon his friend Catwy at Llancarvan; and he has not recited the anecdote about the Saint interposing between King Arthur and a violator of his domestic peace who had availed himself of the monastic asylum of Glastonbury. He merely stales that Gildas passed his closing years there, and was buried within its precincts, without making any allusion to the rival claims of Rhwys in Armorica.

When, ascending to the preceding generation, William comes to St. Patrick, his statements, being unfamiliar to most readers, will appear to jar, not only with the account which is now generally accepted, but even with the notions which were prevalent in the twelfth and subsequent centuries. His statements are to this effect:—that when St. Germanus had by his visit to South Britain quelled the Pelagian heresy there, and was returning to his own diocese of Auxerre, Patrick was one of the British youths whom he selected and took with him; that after some years' training in his school, Patrick

THE HOLY GRAIL

was consecrated a bishop and sent to effect the evangelization of Ireland, a work which he successfully accomplished; that after many years he demitted his primatial office, and returned to his own country, landing on the Cornish beach; that having entered the Island Valley of Glastonia, he induced twelve hermits whom he found there to form a congregation or community to which he imparted a rule of discipline; that he passed his closing years as their Superior or Abbot, and was finally buried within the old Church in which they performed their devotions.

Now, many Ecclesiologists, including such authorities as Lanigan and Todd, holding fast the tradition that the great missionary started on his voyage to Ireland either from Boulogne or from Al-Clwvyd (=Dumbarton); that he passed the remainder of his life in his See of Armagh, and that he was buried at Sabhal or Downpatrick, have pronounced the preceding statements to be figments, contrived to promote the credit and influence of Glastonbury. The fact, however, is that William's account is open to objection only because it is crude in its form, and fails to discriminate its subject from another person who bore the same name and performed a similar part in Irish history. A later Glastonbury Chronicler has noticed two Patricii as associated with Ireland, and distinct from the Patricius of Auvergne. His account, indeed, by itself is of little significance, but what is of for greater moment, the oldest Irish authorities—biographies, hymns, and annals, ranging from the eighth (if not the seventh) to the tenth or eleventh century—concur in distributing the conversion of the Island between three eminent missionaries. These were Palladius, also called Patricius, the Legate of Pope Celestine I., who in less than a year abandoned his task, and went over to Caledonia; Succath, also called Patricius, who, though a volunteer, spent all the latter part of his life in achieving the

MEDIÆVAL LEGENDS

work initiated by the Legate, and so has been accredited with his apostolic attributes; and an evangelist older than either, by some represented as the teacher of Succath, who is distinguished by the title *Patricius Senior* or *Senex* =Senpatrick, or Patrick the Elder, and who, after he had for many years filled the See of Armagh, departed into South Britain, settled in the monastery Glassenbyri or Glastonia, and is, therefore, designated *Abbas* (or sometimes *Episcopus*) *Glastoniensis*. While these three Patricks are often inextricably confused, the acts and fortunes of each being ascribed to one of the others, their dates are fairly determined. The date of Senpatrick's advent seems uncertain, but his death is recorded in the Annals of Ulster in A.D. 457, in the Annals of Connaught A.D. 454.* The brief visit of Palladius was about 431-2, and the life-long work of Succath from 433 till 492.

In regard to the localities from which they started upon their missions, the conflicting notices might be reconciled by the surmise that Palladius, a Gaul, perhaps of Auvergne, sailed from Boulogne, or some other Continental port, Succath from Menthur, identified with Al-Clwyd or Dumbarton, and Senpatrick from the Southern or Western coast of Britain, between the Land's End and Cardigan Bay.

It may be added that some of the Irish documents, far older than William's compilation, confirm his statement that Benignus or Benean, successor of Patricius (Sen-Patrick) at Armagh, likewise retired in due course to Glastonbury, and there became the second Abbot. Further, William's assertion

---

* Archbishop Ussher quotes the record of his death from the Annals or Connaught, and adds, as evidence of his connection with Glastonbury, the statement in the Life of Dunstan that pilgrims from Ireland resorted there in honour of *beati Patricii Senioris, qui faustus ibidem in Domino quievisse narratur. De Brit. Eccles. Primordiis*, p. 895.

that the cloisters which had been hallowed by the presence, and the remains of those venerated inmates continued through subsequent ages to be visited by crowds of Irish pilgrims is fully borne out, on the one hand by a biography of St. Dunstan, written in the tenth century, which tells of that renowned Saint having received instruction in childhood and youth from Irish monks and devotees, who frequented the Abbey which he was destined to rule, and on the other hand by the glossary of Cormac, composed in the ninth century, which distinguishes "a Church on the border of the Jetian Sea," though bearing the Saxon name "*Glasimpere*" as belonging not to the Saxons (*Gaill*) but to the Irish, "*Glasimpere nan Gaedel.*"

If the two letters which bear the name of Patricius, the *Confessio* or autobiography, and the *Epistola in Coroticum* or arraignment of the marauding Prince of Cardigan, were written by Sen-Patrick (which may be the case, though some of the Irish authorities assume them to belong to Succath), the two visits to Ireland described in the former, to which William,— to whom those letters were probably unknown,—has made no allusion, must be conceived to have been facts accomplished when the still vigorous though now experienced missionary was introduced to St. Germanus. The topographical notices in those documents have not been identified by critical research, but they are at any rate as suitable to localities in Southern and Western Britain as to any in other quarters which have been suggested. The oldest of extant British Chronicles, compiled by Marcus the Eremite, Nennius and others in the eighth and ninth centuries, which gives us Patrick's vernacular name "Maun" or "Mawon" (sometimes Latinised Magonius), adding that he received that of Patricius at his consecration, passes over the interval between his return from captivity in Ireland and the period of his studies on the Continent, but it makes him land in Britain, and make a short stay there, before proceeding to Ireland in pursuance of the mission which had been entrusted to him as the successor of Palladius. In a Life of the Cornish Saint Guinger, written in the eleventh century, and attributed to Archbishop Anselm, his landing is said to have been in Cornwall, and his departure from that district for Ireland to have been accelerated by a supernatural warning. By Ricemarchus, Bishop of St. Asaph in the eleventh century, followed by Giraldus Cambrensis and others, he is described as lingering in Cardigan (*Kereticam regionem*), Dyved or Pembroke (*Demetica rura*), and as resolving to pass a life of devotion in the charming Vale of Rhos (*Rosina Vallis*) near Mynyw (*Menevia*) when an angelic apparition apprised him that that region was reserved for St. David in the next generation, and that he must hasten to the field of glorious labour which awaited him in Ireland.*

The writers just quoted, though they may be said to favour the view that Patrick returned from Ireland into South Britain, inasmuch as they suggest a motive and an explanation of that step in his affection for his native soil, have in nowise asserted that it actually took place.

In certain Genealogies of Silurian Saints, the date of which is undetermined, but probably very recent, Patrick the Apostle of Ireland is claimed as a native of Gwyr (=Gower) in South Glamorgan, and is said to have been the first Principal, or at any rate a teacher in the most famous Cor or Bangor (=Choir or College) in that district—viz., the one at Caer-Worgorn or Worgan. That College was really founded about A.D. 490 by Dubricius (Dyvrig), the first Bishop of Llandaff, and had for its first President the Armorican Monk-Knight Iltutus (Illtud Varchawg), after whom it was styled Bangor-Illtud or

---

*These writers are quoted by Abp. Ussher, De Brit. Eccles, Primordiis, C.XVII., pp. 843-5.

THE HOLY GRAIL

Llan-Illtud Vawr (a name clipped and translated nowadays Llantwit Major), and it continued to flourish till the time of the Norman invasion. But in order that it might be associated with more exalted patrons, its origin was pushed back to the time of St. Germanus and his pupil Patricius, the Emperor Theodosius I. (*Tewdws*), and the beatified Constantine (*Cystennin Vendigaid*) King of Cornwall. The Cor Tewdws established under Imperial auspices by Balerus (=Valerius), "a man from Rome," was soon burnt down by Irish invaders (Gwyddel), and the Bangor Illtud was not erected upon its site till after a lapse of forty years. Its Principal Padrig, of Dano-Irish lineage, named also Mawon (as in Nennius), or Maenwin or Son of Maenwin, was carried off by the marauders across the sea, and he repaid them by the conversion of their Island to the Christian faith. Now, by describing Patrick when he was made captive as an abbot or a teacher, instead of a stripling as in the older accounts of his life [and in the *Confessio* which is generally believed to have been written by himself], this story loses in probability as in external support, and it is at variance with the tradition that he had returned from Ireland before he filled an abbatial office in his own country. Indeed one historic notice based upon these genealogies affirms that he did not return from Ireland at all, but died there at his post and in harness; and the upshot of what has been said is that the special claim of Glastonbury to have been his final home, strongly supported by the oldest Irish documents, receives no additional confirmation from Cambrian sources.*

Let us return to the Glastonian account of twelve Solitaries, whom, according to it, St. Patrick found in Ynys Wydrin, and organised as members of a Monastic College. They are stated

---

* Iolo MSS. collected by Edward Williams, Llandovery, 1848, pp. 455-6, 500, 534, 537.

MEDIÆVAL LEGENDS

to have succeeded to twelve others, and a continuous series of Solitaries, twelve and twelve, was traced back in the same locality to the latter half of the second century. At that time, as we are told, a British King (*Llwrwg* or *Llevr Mawr*) sent commissioners to Rome and induced Pope Eleutherius to send back with them missionaries to instruct him and his people in Christian faith and practice. The papal missionaries, headed by Damianus and Faganus (Dwyvan and Fagan), were eminently successful in converting, baptizing, and educating the Britons, and having entered the marshy district of Ynys Wydrin, they renovated the ancient and venerated church of wattled work, dedicated to the Virgin Mother, which they had discovered in the plain; and over against it upon the Tor (a spur of the Mendip Hills) they erected an oratory to Michael the Archangel. Here they remained nine years, and left twelve of their associates in the vicinity of the Old Church, and, availing themselves of the King's bounty, they made provision for a perpetual succession of ascetics, neither more nor fewer than twelve at a time,—the last group of whom was organised, as we have already seen, into a monastic congregation by St. Patrick.

Here it may be observed that no definite locality in Britain was associated with King Lucius in the old and meagre accounts of him transmitted from the fourth or fifth century, and repeated by Beda and Nennius, and it is only when we come down to the twelfth century that we find indications of his ordinary place of residence in writings drawn up in the vicinity of the Bristol Channel, in which writings he is, of course, connected with the same quarter of the Island. Thus the Glastonians, as has just been shown, imply that he exercised authority in North Somerset. Their contemporary Geoffry of Monmouth, in his elaborate version of the Legend, says that he died in his capital *Glaudiocestra*, or Gloucester; and the compilers of the *Liber Landavensis* (of about the same date)

THE HOLY GRAIL

fix his seat of government in Gwent, including Monmouth and Glamorgan, and represent him as founding the oldest church, (by which is meant cathedral), in Britain at Llandaff.

It was however natural that a ruler, who was so much looked up to by the native tribes beyond the pale of the Roman Province as to be commonly spoken of as Monarch of the Britons, should be regarded as having by his example and encouragement, if not by his direct influence, promoted the spread of the religion which he had espoused, outside of, as well as within, his own dominions. Hence two Missionaries sent to him from Rome, Damianus and Faganus, whose names appear as first and second in the long roll of the bishops of Llandaff, were averred in tradition to have also, about A.D. 167, founded the See of Somerset, not indeed at Wells,—to which it was transferred by its last British occupant with the concurrence of Ina in 721,—but at a place nearer Glastonbury, which long afterwards acquired the name Congresbury from an abbot of a monastery there, Congarus (Cyngar), also named Docuinus, a contemporary of Dubricius, who, about A.D. 474, left it with twelve of his monks and founded another monastery in Glamorganshire. Again, the third bishop of Llandaff was according to one statement Medwy or Medwin "a Belgian," one of the two worthies who had carried the petition of Lucius to the Pope, from whom they received ordination, while the other, Elvan "an Avalonian," was alleged by later writers to have founded at Glastonbury itself a Cor (=Choir) or monastic school, which was looked upon as the precursor of the Bangor or College presided over by St. Patrick,—in the same fashion as at Caer-Worgan, the Institute ruled by St. Patrick, was the precursor of the more complex organism constructed by St. Illtud.

This conception, obscuring the statement that an eremitic system had continued in Ynys Wydrin till the fifth century, obtained wide acceptance; and the monastery there, with others in Saxonised districts, came to be classed with those within the Principality as if permanently upon the same footing with them. Thus one of the so-called Historical Triads (Cambro. Brit. II., 386), compiled about the fifteenth century, brackets, as if coexisting within telescopic view, "the three *Cyvangors* chief Perpetual Choirs of the Isle of Britain: Bangor Illtyd Varchawg in Caer Worgorn, Cor Emyrs in Caer Caradawg (=Ambresbury near Old Sarum) and the Bangor of Gwydrin in the Isle of Avallen." Thus, in regard to the locality of the operations favoured by King Lucius, the accounts current at Glastonbury and those in the Diocese of Llandaff were more in accord than we found them to be in the case of St. Patrick.

Now it would have been irrelevant to the subject of the present work to discuss even cursorily the Glastonian traditions recorded by the well-read and discreet Monk of Malmesbury, had he, after tracing them up to the latter half of the second century, been permitted by his clients to rest and be thankful on that conspicuous height. For his own part he doubtless felt that he had then ascended at least as far as was warranted by the evidences submitted to him, even if these were scanned with indulgence and exempted from rude criticism. But he had admitted without challenge,—though not, it may be, without misgivings,—certain grants and charters of Ini and other West Saxon rulers, which, although endorsed by various kings of England, Norman as well as Saxon, are manifestly spurious, and a yet more outrageous fabrication entitled a letter of St. Patrick (*Charta Patricii*), which intimates, in vague but unmistakable terms, that the British history of "the Old Church" and of its monastic Congregation began long before the reign of Lucius. It was acknowledged by all his authorities that the papal missionaries, when they penetrated Ynys Wydrin, found it an utter wilderness abandoned by man and tenanted only by wild beasts; but then it was added that within its circuit they discovered a venerable church, the oldest in Britain, which had been raised by some of the first disciples of Christ in obedience to an angelic monition, and had been consecrated by our Lord Himself. It was affirmed also that good evidence met them, in the form of Christian relics and ancient records, that there twelve anchorites, on whom the pagan Princes of the district had bestowed twelve hides of land, had passed their lives in austere seclusion, though no successors had occupied their cells. And thus the work to which the royal Catechumen and his spiritual advisers addressed themselves proved to be only the restoration of what time had effaced or obscured. Of these documentary statements, and of oral testimonies to the same effect, William felt himself called upon to take note, and to offer such explanation as he or his friends could devise. Thus impelled he had to breast yet another steep, to climb yet another century—a hundred years and three, as he has reckoned with painful accuracy,—and to plant the Glastonian standard on the pinnacle of the Apostolic age itself. He has therefore resuscitated the old Isidorian tradition, endorsed by Freculphus in the eight century, about the mission of St. Philip and his disciples into Gaul. Thereupon he remarks that it was only natural that some of those evangelists should visit the British shore, and considering this surmise to be verified by the testimony adduced in St. Patrick's Charter, he finds that those disciples, twelve in number, were the ascetic colonists of the Avalonian Isle. Then tacitly collating with this result information derived from hearsay, or through some undefined channel (*ut ferunt*), he announces, as if an obvious and simple corollary, that the leader of these primitive settlers instructed by St. Philip, and as he sometimes adds St. James (the Less) was no other than "the dearest friend of Philip," Joseph of Arimathaea. Regarding his antecedent and subsequent life he enters into no explanations, but includes him among the twelve whose pious works, especially their building of the Church, and whose death in that sequestered spot he chronicles. And it is worthy of special note that he has appealed to no evidence, whether written or monumental, that Joseph visited Glastonbury or any part of Britain, or even that he was with Philip in Gaul;—whether it was that his informants were unprepared to bring such proofs under his notice, or that mistrusting their genuineness, he could not prevail upon himself to adduce them.

This lack of testimonies has been supplied in some of the works either compiled within the great abbey or receiving their inspiration from it; such as the large Tablet or folding screen long preserved there; the Chronicle by an anonymous monk written about A.D. 1259; that by Adam of Domerham about A.D. 1300; that by John of Glastonbury about A.D. 1400; the Legend Books compiled by John of Tinmouth, a monk of St. Albans, about 1360, and by John Capgrave, an Augustinian of Canterbury who lived from 1393 to 1464. Two other authorities are referred to in the documents which embody the Glastonbury legend, namely "the Book found in the *Praetorium* of Pilatus by the Emperor Theodosius," and "the Book which is called *Graal* or *Sanctum Graal*." The former is the *Acta Pilati* or *Evangelium Nicodemi*, which has been fully discussed in chapter II., and it leaves Joseph still in Jerusalem or Judaea after his liberation from prison. The history and contents of the latter work, the *Graal* or *Sanctum Graal*, are presently to occupy our attention. It undoubtedly treats of the migrations of the Arimathaean family, and, in the recension known to Capgrave, it describes the arrival of Joseph, his wife and his son Josephes in Britain; but it, in all except the latest versions, locates their sojourning and adventures in Wales, and thus fails to supply a groundwork for the pretensions of Glastonbury.

THE HOLY GRAIL

This last remark suggests a query whether those pretensions were at all interfered with by rival claims advanced in other districts of Britain, especially in South Wales, where as we have already seen views were entertained which partially confirmed but materially modified the Glastonian traditions regarding both the action of King Lucius, and the connexion of St. Patrick with South Western Britain. Considering the account given in some recensions of the Book of the Graal regarding the movements of Joseph in Gower or South Wales, we might have expected to find an affirmative answer to this query in some of the documents which were collected in the Book of Llandaff in the course of the twelfth century. As it is, the earliest notice, evidently implying a compromise between theories current on the two sides of the British Channel, occurs in the Pedigree of Iestyn ab Gwrgan, a prince of Glamorgan whose death is dated A.D. 1086, and this Pedigree, which quotes a work composed between 1450 and 1490, is probably to be dated in the sixteenth century. This notice, as edited and translated by Edward and Taliesin Williams (Iolo MSS., pp. 7=343-4), states that Eurgain, daughter of Caradog (=Caractacus), brought with her from Rome, or induced to come after her, Ilid "a native of the land of Israel," to aid her in proselytising her countrymen to the Christian faith which she had adopted. Now this "Ilid" is called in the service of his Commemoration "St. Joseph of Arimathaea." He became the principal teacher of Christianity to the Cambro-Britons, and introduced good order into the choir of Eurgain, which she had established for twelve saints near the place now called Llantwit.* After this arrangement "Ilid went to *Ynys Afallon*=the Isle of Apples, in the Summer

---

* It is added that this Coir of Eurgain was burnt in the time of King Edgar.

MEDIÆVAL LEGENDS

Country (Somersetshire), where he died and was buried; and Ina, King of that country, raised a large church over his grave, at the place now called *Glasinbyri*, in Welsh Aberglaston."

The Eurgain or Eigen mentioned above, with her husband—here styled a Roman noble, but elsewhere named Sarllog, Lord of Caer Sarllog (=Old Sarum)—have been identified with the British Lady Claudia, and her Roman husband Pudens, repeatedly mentioned by Martial, who again have been recognised in the Claudia and Pudens mentioned by St. Paul (2 Tim., IV. 21). Some incongruities in this hypothesis would be lessened if Claudia were supposed not to have been the same with Eurgain, or a daughter of Caractacus at all, but of a different family, (that of Cogidunus has been suggested), though she may have been on intimate terms with the family of the Silurian Chief and have returned to Britain in their company.

Laying that question aside, it concerns us to note only the outcome of the statements made in the above Pedigree, in various genealogies of Cambrian saints, compiled probably about the same time, and in two of the so-called historic Triads which may likewise be dated in the fifteenth or sixteenth century: it is this, that Bran=Brennus, father of Caradog or Caractacus, and his granddaughter Eurgain, having become Christians during a seven years stay as hostages at Rome, on their return to Siluria, brought over as evangelists Arwystli Hen "a man of Italy," Ilid "a man of Israel," or "from the land of Israel," and another "Man of Israel" Cyndav Hen, with his son Mawan or Meugaut. Of these names the first is believed to represent (not Ariobistulus, but) Aristobulus,—this very Arwystli Hen being identified with the Aristobulus of St. Paul's Epistle to the Romans (Rom. XVI. 10);—the second is of uncertain origin, not being a scriptural name, unless perhaps corrupted from *Eliud* (which remains unchanged in

THE HOLY GRAIL

some Welsh lists), nor yet obviously a British one;—the third and fourth are unmistakably Kymric. Each of them was borne also by persons of much later date who are commemorated by churches and chapelries; and indeed Cyndav and Mawan are themselves by several authorities placed in the second, or the sixth, or even a later century, and said to have come from Armorica.

One, however, of the chapels known as Llanilid, in Glamorganshire, described as the oldest in Britain, is understood to commemorate the associate of the princess Eurgain. She is said to have founded a Choir or College of twelve monastic brethren somewhere in Gwent, called after herself Cor Eurgain, and placed at its head Ilid, by whom she had been converted, and whom she looked up to as her director, while Bran, her grandfather, was guided by Arwystli. The site usually named is Caer Worgan,—her Cor being supposed to have been restored and developed in the Cor Tewdws, regulated by St. Patrick, and afterwards reorganised on a grander scale in the Bangor Illtud,—so called from Illtud, the friend of Dubricius.*

Thus far all the Silurian notices agree; but the Pedigree of Iestyn appears to be solitary in adding that Ilid at last changed his abode for Ynys Wydrin, and was the same with the founder of the society there, which was afterwards organised as the Cor Elvan, and vastly enlarged as the Bangor Wydrin. The compiler of this Pedigree,—whoever he was, and at whatever time he lived, (for unfortunately all documents which have no other warrant than that of Iolo Morganwg lie under a cloud of suspicion), may have come upon a tradition that Ilid closed his life and was buried in Glastonbury, the founding of which he knew to be ascribed to Joseph of Arimathaea,

---

* Iolo. MSS., pp. 538-9, 550, 555, 557-8.

MEDIÆVAL LEGENDS

and having remarked that Ilid's commemoration day in the Silurian Kalendar was (for we will assume it to have been so) March 17, being the day dedicated to the Arimathaean by the Latin Church, as July 31 is by the Greeks, and putting together the two circumstances he may have formed a surmise, which he treated as a discovery, that the Gwentian Ilid and the Glastonian Joseph were one and the same person. This compromise between a Silurian legend and their own the chroniclers of Glastonbury do not seem to have anywhere alluded to; and we may be quite sure that if it had been proposed, they would have repudiated the suggestion that the isapostolic Founder of their society had come to Britain, and passed his best days there, as the satellite of a Silurian princess.

Yet while strictly guarding his venerated name and ideal, those chroniclers, as appears from the previous abstract, did not seek to "rise to the height of this great argument," and did not take even ordinary pains to vindicate his title by assigning to him traits or actions distinct from those of his most eminent successors. Presenting to us rather a chronological series than a historic tablet, discriminating names rather than characters, epochs rather than events, they have not even by a scantling of invention courted assent to their assumption that a band of twelve ascetics in the first century formed the germ of an Institution, which, though hidden for a while, reappeared in the second century, and bloomed afresh in the sixth, or that Joseph, the delegate of Philip, was more than a pale reflection or foreshadowing of Elvan or of Patrick.

At the same time, though repetitions might have been to some extent disguised, coincidences between legends of Joseph and legends of Patrick would remain; and some are discovered, not only in those of Glastonbury and Gwent, but also in legends which were rife in quite different localities. Little stress need be laid upon the fact that the same feast

THE HOLY GRAIL

day was assigned to Joseph and to Ilid, and to several of the saints who bore the name or title of Patricius,—to Palladius, to Succath, to Patricius of Auvergne, and Patricius of Nola. It is more curious to find St. Patrick of Ireland spoken of in one of his oldest biographies as of Jewish descent, just as Ilid, and even Cyndav Hen are often called "men of Israel;" and again that the extirpation of all venomous reptiles from the Irish soil, for which the great missionary is celebrated, is attributed in at least one legend to Joseph of Arimathaea.

CHAPTER VIII.

Glastonbury, the Burial Place of Saints and Heroes.

REMEMBERING the importance which, in determining the selection of tutelar Saints, was always attached to such monumental, or otherwise trustworthy evidence as could be adduced to prove that the personage, who was claimed by the nation or district as the primitive evangelist, was really interred in some spot within its territory, we might have expected to hear of a very early and strenuous endeavour to discover the tombs of Joseph and his eleven companions at Glastonbury. But the fact is that the earliest practical steps that we find on record towards such exploration in the cemetery of the Abbey were dictated by political, and especially dynastic considerations rather than by ecclesiastical pretensions.

They were prompted by a desire to ascertain the resting place of the far-famed King Arthur, in whom his Cambrian compatriots continued to assert an exclusive interest, but whom the dominant Normans had come to look upon as one of the mighty dead, who on quitting this mortal coil had shaken off the trammels of race and party,—whom they could include in their own wide sympathies,—whose renown they would foster as that of an adopted ancestor, and whose protection they might hope to share with their British and Saxon neighbours.

It is well known that both in Britain and on the continent, during the twelfth and thirteenth centuries, the Cymri maintained that no sepulchre of Arthur had ever been found, and questioned, or explicitly denied, that the wounds he had received on the field of Camlan had proved fatal, holding that in

THE HOLY GRAIL

the mystic Isle to which he had been then conveyed, his state remained that of a semiconscious life in death, and that he might be expected, when the destined period should arrive, to return to his beloved people, whose wrongs he would redress, and to whom he would restore ascendancy over all their rivals. The Norman and Anjevin rulers were of course anxious to counteract a delusion so fraught with mischief and peril, and it appeared to them a promising expedient to devise some way of inducing those who were under this delusion to accept a typical or spiritual interpretation of the old bardic prophecies which favoured it, as implying no more than that a deliverer was about to come in the spirit and power of Arthur,—not indeed of his lineage, but ready to give effect to his purest aspirations. The course might be cleared, as they imagined, for such a hypothesis by a demonstration that the "Avalon" to which he had retired was a district which had long passed under Saxon, and then under Norman sway, that he was there really entombed within the precincts of a Normanised Abbey, and that his grave was revered by the present rulers, even more deeply than by their predecessors.

The first of the Plantagenet Kings, Henry II., was just the man likely from his character and position to be attracted by a project apparently conducive to the policy of uniting the British Isles under a single sceptre,—a policy which he very early sketched out, and to which amid all difficulties he tenaciously adhered. Soon after his accession, A.D. 1155, he obtained from Adrian II., the only English-born Pope, a grant of the Lordship of Ireland, and from his successor, Alexander III., a confirmation of that grant; and though troubles at home and entanglements abroad long prevented him from availing himself of the advantage thus secured, he in 1171 passed six months in Ireland, personally directing a campaign which extended and consolidated the conquests previously made by

MEDIÆVAL LEGENDS

Strongbow, his Lieutenant. In 1174 he wrung from his captive, William the Lion, at Falaise, a deed of submission and fealty for the Kingdom of Scotland,—a deed which his son Richard I. cancelled in 1189, on receiving a large sum of money.

To repress the chronic turbulence of the Welsh tribes, whom the Lords of the Western Marches were unable to keep in subjection, he in 1157, 1163, and 1165 penetrated their mountain barriers, and in 1184 had reached Gloucester on his way to make a fourth inroad, when he received the timely submission of the chiefs in revolt. It has been surmised that his ill-fated grandchild, the son of Geoffry of Anjou and Constance of Bretagne, received at Nantes in 1187 the baptismal name Arthur, in the hope that the Continental Britons might be won over to recognise in their future Duke that long expected leader whose advent was destined to fulfil the predictions of Myrddin, and the other seers of Wales. It is reported that Henry, during one of his Welsh campaigns, received from a native minstrel some hints which induced him to consult the authorities of Glastonbury as to a feasible mode of turning the traditions of that Abbey to good account.

It is rather remarkable that during the long period—about half a century—while the abbey was vested in the hands of Henry de Blois, Bishop of Winchester, for some time Papal Legate, and the most influential churchman of his day, a brother of King Stephen and a Norman of the Normans, no measures appear to have been adopted with a view to carry out this project. Similarly blank in regard to Arthurian discoveries was the abbacy of Roger of Winchester from 1171 to 1178, and so was the interregnum from 1178 to 1189, though during that period King Henry, appropriating the revenues, rebuilt in statelier style the minster and chapels reared about 970 by King Edgar under the guidance of St. Dunstan, which had been burnt down in 1184. In his new Charter of 1185 he

THE HOLY GRAIL

endorsed the extravagant fictions and confirmed the ample privileges which had been set forth in the Charters ascribed to St. Patrick, King Ini, and other benefactors. If we accept as most probable the date of June 1189, for the death of Henry II., and that of the ensuing September for the installation as Abbot of his nephew, or near kinsman, Henry of Soilly (Solliacum), or of Swansea, and if the latter was already Abbot, when the search so long deferred was at length made, then the discovery did not after all gild the close of the eventful reign of Henry Fitzempress, but auspiciously ushered in that of his successor *Cœur de Lion*,—whether in the last months of 1189, or in 1190, or even 1191. The discrepancies as to details and dates among the authorities upon this subject,—and especially between two acute and well-informed writers, both of whom were closely connected with the Court, Gerald Barry and Matthew Paris,—are very puzzling; but they all concur as to the main fact, that in a deep grave within the cemetery of the laity, between two stone pyramids which are frequently referred to, the bodies of Arthur, and Guinevere his second wife, (later authors have chosen to add that of Modred) were duly found, and more than certified by means of epitaphs and distinctive tokens, were translated to the great church recently erected, and were there reposited beneath the high altar. Gerald, as he himself tells us, saw some of the bones shortly afterwards. In 1277 or 1278 the greatest of the Plantagenets, Edward I., with his Queen Eleanor, visited the tomb which was reopened, inspected the royal remains,—commemorating the event by a new inscription, and confirming in a new Charter the immunities and possesions of the abbey.

Whether the political results of the Abbot Henry's achievement were such as fully satisfied the anticipations of his patrons may be open to question, but there can be no doubt that it was highly gratifying to the monastic authorities, who

MEDIÆVAL LEGENDS

accordingly blazoned its details in their archives and added to the treatise of William, with which many liberties had been already taken, a section in which the tradition of their predecessors was transmuted into an authenticated fact. Yet they quite naturally regarded the success which had been realised as affording avantage ground for the attainment of an object which they held to be of yet higher value.

Religious Brotherhoods in Mediæval Europe, as well as throughout Eastern Asia, conceived that a pre-eminent Saint, and influential missionary was,—what the Stoics predicated of their Sage,—a veritable King, and highly as they might prize the tutelage of a Royal convert sepulchred among them, they attached more moment to the possession of relics which assured to them the continued protection of a great teacher, from whom their faith and discipline had been transmitted. At the same time, the competition among various communities for such a heritage rendered the adjudication of it to anyone of them more difficult, and in a proportionate degree enhanced its value. With whatever pride and pleasure the undisputed tomb of Edgar was pointed out at Glastonbury, it was the acquisition of St. Dunstan's bones, though avowedly by questionable means, which was most zealously asseverated,—which kept up for generations an embittered strife between the partisans of Glastonbury and those of Canterbury. Great as was the triumph over popular scepticism which was assured when, in the absence of any rival claims, the coffins of Arthur and Guinevere were brought to light, it would have been considered a higher privilege to be accredited with the custody of the remains of St. Gildas, if the opposition of the Armorican Rhuys could have been bought off. A compromise was reluctantly made in the case of St. Patrick, when it was allowed that, besides the Apostle who died and was buried in his Glastonian Abbey, an evangelist bearing the same name, and living in the same age, had been interred within his Diocese of Armagh. There must have been heart burnings when it was found necessary to concede the superior claims of Welsh and Irish or Scottish sanctuaries to enclose the remains of St. David, St. Columb, St. Benignus, and St. Bridget of Kildare.

The clients of William of Malmesbury could not but be mortified by the vague terms in which their apologist, while adducing the authority of charters in which he could have little confidence, had expressed himself regarding the sepulture of the Anchorites of the first three centuries,—especially the first twelve, whose leader he had indeed assumed to be St. Joseph, but this only in the way of a surmise, which he had not cared to repeat or to confirm. Still for a long time sheer lack of evidence discouraged them from advancing further in the desired direction. So late as A.D. 1259, the author of an anonymous Chronicle, and, about A.D. 1300, Adam of Domerham, in continuing William's account down to A.D. 1290, adhering to the phraseology which had become stereotyped regarding the twelve disciples of Philip and James, still omit any mention of Joseph, as having visited Avalon and died there. But such reticence was felt to be more and more irksome, and various essays were made to secure for the apostolic missionary, in connection with Glastonbury, the same recognition that had been accorded to the patriot king. Not only John of Glastonbury, who continued the narratives of William of Malmesbury and Adam of Domerham down to 1400, but outsiders who professed to have derived their materials from the archives of the Abbey—notably John of Tinmouth, a monk of St. Albans, about 1360, and John Capgrave, an Augustinian of Canterbury, who lived from 1393 to 1464,—concurred in assigning to Joseph the chief place among the original hermits, and in indicating his place of sepulture in the Monks Cemetery.

MEDIÆVAL LEGENDS

In several of these records, and in a famous, though unfortunately undated document, usually styled "the Great Glastonian Tablet,"—being a folding screen composed of wooden leaves covered with parchment, which was preserved in the Abbey till its dissolution,—we find cited two sets of Latin hexameters without author's name or date. One of these sets, a tetrastych with rhyme endings, states that Joseph of Arimathaea with his son Josĕphes (=Josaphat) and ten others entered the Avalonian Vale, and had land in Glastonia assigned to them; while the other, consisting of ten verses four of which are in rhyme, without mentioning Josephes the son, tells how in the year 31 after the Passion (A.D. 63) Joseph commissioned by Philip achieved with his company a miraculous voyage from Gaul to Britain, obtained twelve hides of land from the pagan prince Arviragus for the support of his colony, and caused the famous church of wattled work to be built, as a nucleus of the settlement. There is adduced also a lengthy fragment of a prose Chronicle, attributed to one Melchinus an Avalonian, who is said to have lived earlier than Merlin, perhaps about A.D. 550, and to have been like him a Bard of the prophetic order. The fragment is a turgid rhapsody on the "*Insula Avallonis*," as a cemetery famous from time immemorial. Deeply revered, and frequented by all Kymrian and Gadhelic tribes,—in the same way as the Isle of Enlli or Bardsey off the coast of Caernarvon, and Hy or Iona off the coast of Argyle,—to it were translated in later times from less hallowed and less secure resting places the remains of many Saxons and Angles of note, such as Hilda the Abbess of Whitby; and so, according to this rhapsody it was "decorated with the pearls of prediction by both the heathen of yore and the worshippers of the Most High." If there was any ground for believing that "Avăron," a variant reading for Avalon (which occurs elsewhere), had been known to the writer, he might be considered as having supposed that name to have come from the Latin adjective *avārum*; as it is, he seems to have merely punned upon the first syllable of the name in describing the place as "*avida funeris paganorum*," with an insatiable maw for the corpses of the old pagan settlers,—one of whom, the noblest of all, is declared to repose quietly within its precincts, along with one hundred and four soldiers.

Joseph of Arimathaea is specially dwelt upon, and his place of sepulture is indicated as close to the Oratory reared by the hermits, who are reckoned as not twelve but thirteen. It is averred that "he holds in his sarcophagus two phials of glistening silver filled with the blood and sweat of the prophet Jesus," and it is announced that when that sarcophagus shall once be discovered, and opened up to the public view, the rain and dew of heaven shall never cease to refresh the dwellers in this famous Isle, and, according to this prophet, "These things are to be made manifest long before the dawning of the Day of Doom in the Valley of Jehosaphat."*

Now it is obvious that neither in the nameless verses nor in the rhapsodic prose have we any notes of primitive antiquity. The latter indeed with its "pearls of prediction" is closely analogous to the so-called prophetic poems of the Welsh bards Merddin, Taliesin, Talhaiarn, and others, which give themselves out as productions of the sixth century, but the date of which the criticism of Stephen and Nash has brought down to the twelfth century or later. It would appear that at the time when the passage was concocted, the event which it anticipates as one auspicious to the British Isle, the discovery of St. Joseph's grave, had not yet been attempted, but was seri-

---

* See Joseph of Arimathie, Early English Text Society, London, 1871, Preface, pp. XX.XXI. Notes pp. 69-72; Abp. Ussher, De Brit. Eccles. Primordiis C.II., pp. 16-22.

MEDIÆVAL LEGENDS

ously contemplated. Accordingly, in 1345, a humble petition was drawn up and presented to Edward III. by a citizen of London named John Bloom, requesting the royal sanction to his proposal of a search being made for Joseph's body in the precincts of Glastonbury, as suggested in a revelation which had been vouchsafed to him. The King warmly encouraged the project, on condition of its being agreeable to the Abbey authorities, and expressed his hope that the blessings which the discovery was expected to bring upon the realm might be fully realised. His rescript is remarkable as being the first, perhaps the only, royal document which explicitly recognised the Arimathaean as head of the first twelve Anchorites, while even the forged charters of Ini, and that of Henry II., while speaking of them as the first disciples of Christ on British soil, and as constructors of the oldest oratory here dedicated to the Virgin, had not introduced the name of Joseph,—though it was perhaps in the writer's thoughts and generally understood by readers. From whatever cause, the projected search does not appear to have been actually made, or if made, to have been successful. Long afterwards, under the reign of Elizabeth, the Jesuit William Good is found lamenting that the discovery had not been effected, which would have brought crowds of pilgrims to worship in his native Glastonbury, and to witness numerous miracles there performed. In other writings also, either composed at, or inspired from Glastonbury, some of which go further than Good into details, about the blood-vials and other distinctive tokens, no mention occurs of Joseph's sephulchre as opened up and verified.

Thus left without any tangible evidence that might have excited jubilation, the English authorities in Church and State still betrayed no misgivings, when any historical question sprouted up affecting the early date of the Christianization of Britain. On the contrary, they authorised their delegates,

THE HOLY GRAIL

while disputing for precedence with those of France and Spain, at the General Councils of the Church held at Pisa in 1409, at Constance in 1417, and Basle in 1434, to adduce the Glastonbury Legend in proof that the gospel seed had produced fruit on English soil before it was sown in any other Western clime.* At Constance the representative of Henry V. took up that version of the story which dated the arrival of Joseph and his friends shortly after the Passion; but at Basle the deputy of Henry VI. more discreetly assumed the date A.D. 63, which as we have seen had been accepted in the treatise of William of Malmesbury and in other Glastonbury documents, in conformity with the statement about Philip's arrival in Gaul made by Freeulphus and the other followers of Isidorus. The Spanish deputy Alphonso da Garcia replied on that occasion that while the date A.D. 63 was compatible with the claim of his nation to be the first that accepted the true faith, it, as well as the date put forward at Constance, was refuted by the tradition that Joseph was a close prisoner in Jerusalem until the arrival of Titus or Vespasian, and in reference to the objection to the tradition drawn from the *Evangelium Nicodemi* he offered the same suggestion which, as we have seen, had been advanced by his countryman P. de Natalibus, about 1372, and a century earlier by Jacobus a Voragine, namely that, after the liberation of Joseph on the Resurrection Morn, he might have been again thrown into prison and have remained there till he was liberated by the Roman General.†

But whatever pretensions it might be expedient to flourish in the face of foreign rivals, the time had long passed when

---

* Abp. Ussher gives an account of these disputations, Brit. Eccles. Primordiis C.II., pp. 22-27.

† See chapter V., p. 32, and references in note.

MEDIÆVAL LEGENDS

either dynastic policy or popular sentiment could lead the English nation to contemplate with any seriousness the idea of adopting St. Joseph, or indeed any other Saint, as its Tutelar. A course on which the various races could not agree,—while the memory of Augustine in Kent, of Cuthbert in Northumbria, and of various renowned ascetics of Cambrian and Scotic lineage, was still green,—was not likely to commend itself to an age when the glamour of hagiology was beginning to pale in the light of reviving letters, in the bustle of widening commerce, and amid the novel objects of interest which on all sides attracted attention.

Ireland had been permitted, without a grudge, to appropriate the patronage of St. Patrick, and Wales to nestle under that of St. David. The small Northern Kingdom also, whose conflicting communities had not accepted the common tutelage of a Ninian, or a Kentigern, or a Columba, had in the ninth century united in choosing as its patron Saint the Apostle Andrew, although he was never alleged to have trodden the Caledonian soil, simply because bones, supposed to be his, had been conveyed from Achaia to the coast of Fife, and there reposited as a palladium. England had dispensed with such visionary patronage until it outgrew any general belief in its efficacy, and was quite willing either to forego the name of an advantage which it had ceased to consider a reality, or to allow its rulers, if such were their will, to entrust to a shadow or a semblance a function which was felt to be so vague and unsubstantial.

The early Crusaders had found the cult of a military martyr, styled by the Greeks *Megalomartyr* and *Tropaiophoros*, highly popular in Palestine. By their influence it was diffused in Western Europe, and was brought into England by *Cœur de Lion*. The feast day of St. George, April 23, was recognised in England in 1222, though he was not supposed to have

THE HOLY GRAIL

been connected in either life or death with this country, and though his birthplace, actions, and character were not clearly ascertained.* In 1330, a brand-new order of knighthood was instituted, and that enigmatic saint was nominated as its patron. His device on the national banner, and his name in the liturgy extended his reputation from the Court through wider circles, and at last he was, without protest and almost without observation, placed in the niche which had been left vacant in the presence of saints of an austerer type, and of far older celebrity. Thus heraldry achieved a result which neither devotion nor hagiology had secured; and the irony of history is curiously illustrated when we find that the Sovereign, who in 1330 dedicated his new Order of the Garter to the Lydian or Cappadocian martyr, was the same King Edward III., who in 1345 very graciously received,—though perhaps he took no active steps to further its object,—the petition that the sepulchre of the Arimathaean should be searched for in Glastonbury in the hope that its discovery would draw down priceless blessings upon the English realm.

---

* Notes, Note 15.

APPENDIX TO CHAPTER IV.

The Earlier History of Pilate.

THE marked popularity and wide diffusion throughout Western Europe, in the twelfth and thirteenth centuries, of the narratives regarding the latter days of Pilate explain the favour generally accorded to various attempts which were made to supply a complete biography of the Procurator by prefixing fancy sketches of his birth, education, and early history. Hardly any reference to these sketches appears to have made its way into any work generally accessible, and the reader may be disposed to welcome a brief notice of their outlines, as an appendix to our episodical chapter.

The chief sources of information are the Latin narrations in prose and in verse, of the twelfth century, entitled *Pilatus*, which have been already noticed (pp. 20-30), along with a French version of the prose piece belonging to the thirteenth century; also a German poem entitled "Pilatus," of the twelfth century, and an English poem bearing the same title, probably composed late in the thirteenth century.*

A statement that Lugdunum or Lyon was the birthplace of Pilate, as well as his city of exile, has been recorded by Petrus Comestor in the twelfth century, and repeated in the thirteenth by Jacobus a Voragine:—"*reportatus est in exilium Lugdunum, unde oriundus fuerat.*"† And it re-appears in a

---

* See Schönbach, ll. pp. 186-190; Du Méril, ll. pp. 343-357; ibid, pp. 359-368; H. F. Massman, *Deutsche Gedichte des Zwölften Jahrhunderts u.s.w.* Quedlinburg und Leipzig, 1837, pp. 145-152; F. J. Furnivall, Early English Poems and Lives of Saints, &c., Berlin, 1862, pp. 111-118.

† P. Comestor ap. Vincent, Bellovac. *Speculum Historiale*, T. VIII.,

THE HOLY GRAIL

Mystère de la Passion, entitled *La Vengeance Nostre Seigneur Jesucrist,* where Pilate says of himself,

> "Ceux de Lyon, devans sung homme
> Par an a la cité de Romme
> Me baillèrent a leur plaisance, &c."

But most of our extant notices make him a native of the Rhine land, of Teutonic or Bavarian lineage, connected with Forcheim or Bamberg, or emphatically Mainz (Moguntiacum). The probability is that he was the son of a Roman officer serving in Lower Germany, bearing the same name and surname, Pontius Pilatus, while the prename of each has been forgotten. But no such idea has occurred to the composers of the legend. On the contrary the young German bears the single name Pilatus, which is grotesquely explained as a compound of Pila, the name of his mother, and Atus, the name of either his father or his maternal grandfather.

According to the different narrators, who vary very slightly in their story, though they differ very much in style, Pilate was the natural son of a king of Mainz named Tirus,—if not Atus, on this point our authorities differ,—and of a miller's daughter, near whose cottage the King found himself belated one starry night, when hunting in the adjacent forest. A poetic account is given, especially in the German poem, of the cirumstances in which the royal stargazer sought and obtained the favour of the rustic maid, having read in the heavens that a son begotten by him that night was predestined to hold a high place of power, and to be heard of in many lands.[*]

When the child had grown up to boyhood he was re-

---

c. 124, and *Legenda Aurea* c. LIII., p. 234.

[*] The legendary nativity of Charlemagne was embellished with similar prognostics.

MEDIÆVAL LEGENDS

claimed by his father, and brought to the court. There he killed his legitimate brother with whom he was brought up, and was in consequence sent off as a hostage to Rome, where he next killed a fellow hostage, a son of the king of France, "*un noble enfant né de Franche,*" in another version, a son of the king of England. He was therefore despatched to the Isle of Pontus to quell the turbulence of its barbarous inhabitants. From his success there he acquired the title Pontius, which is treated in this story as a surname equivalent to Ponticus, after the analogy of Asiaticus, Illyricus, &c. Afterwards, by proved ability and unscrupulous finesse, he obtained the government of Judæa independently of Herod, with whom he soon afterwards returned to amity at the trial of Christ, as is recorded in the Canonical Gospels.

The German poem *Pilatus*, published by H. F. Massman, which gives the most picturesque account of Pilate's birth and boyhood, opens with a long invocation to the Virgin, naming her "*ein reht Rosa an Dorn,*" a rose blooming on the thorny Jewish stem. It is printed from a unique MS., and it breaks off just where Pilate is summoned to the help of Herod in his hard task in Judæa.

The French translation from Latin, and the Latin poem, printed by Ed. du Meril, contain the whole story of the shipwrecked messenger, and the cure of Vespasian, as told in the *Vindicta Salvatoris*,* and of Pilate's miserable end. The Latin poet, in parts of his story, seems to indulge in a vein of satire very unusual in such legendary compositions. One can hardly think him serious in his description of the ship laden with

---

* See Chapter IV., pp. 24-26. In this version of the story the messenger comes, not to Titus in Aquitania, but to Vespasian in Galiscia "*en Galisce*"—as the French writer notes,—"*la u li Crestiien requièrent Monsignor Saint Jacqueme.*"

THE HOLY GRAIL

relics, and the procession of clergy, sent down the Rhone from Lyons to Vienne, in search of the dangerous obstruction in the river caused by Pilate's corpse.

It remains to be noticed that in the *Grand Roman du Saint Greal* there occurs an episode, which seems there rather incongruous, and which is manifestly indebted to this Pilate-Legend, announcing that Evelac was the son of a cobbler in Meaux, that he was sent to Rome among other hostages for the fealty of France, that he was afterwards sent by the Emperor into Syria, where he ingratiated himself with Felix, the governor, whose son he killed in a quarrel, and that finally, thanks to his prowess and talents, he became King of Sarras.* Perhaps this plagiarism may suggest that, in one of the French recensions of the Pilate story, instead of Mayence there was named Meaux, or L'Isle de France.

---

* Le Saint Graal, ed. E. Hucher, Tome II., pp. 210-12; and The History of the Holy Grail, English, by H. Lonelich, ed. F. J. Furnivall, London, 1874, Part I., pp. 104-7.

APPENDIX TO CHAPTER VI., SECTION II.

Sequel of the Provençal Legend.

AS in the case of Spain, and in other instances where an eminent Saint, or one of the Apostles, was claimed as Tutelar of the province or the community, we have seen how necessary it was held that his memory should be indissolubly associated with some well-known religious Foundation, and that he should be recognised as occupying some definite sepulchre within his patrimony; so too, in the case of Provence, such a confirmation of the Legend must have appeared to its supporters a thing to be most earnestly and zealously sought for.

The evidence for the connection between certain Provençal churches or abbeys and the missionaries from Bethany was always felt to be but hazy; and, what is far more significant, the claims of Marseilles, Aix, and Tarascon to preserve the remains of Lazarus and his sisters were strongly contested in those very centuries—the eleventh, twelfth, and thirteenth—during which such claims engrossed the deepest interest. Such was the case even while Marseilles kept up a constant intercourse with the ports of Syria and Egypt, while pilgrims, soldier-monks, and crusading hosts were incessantly astir on the highway and on the sea, while the cult of Lazarus, patron of warriors and wayfarers, of Martha, model of housewives and typical sister of mercy, and of the Magdalene, holiest and austerest of penitents, exercised its magnetic influence over throngs of votaries. The lack of such monumental testimonies as it was the custom to adduce could not fail to suggest misgivings, even to those whose faith in an interesting narrative was in no way qualified by its inherent improbability, and those by whom the marvellous was most lovingly credited for its own sake. Some apology then for the lack was indispensable. At the same time there were in vogue three conflicting hypotheses as to the locality in which the Bethanians attained their final resting place; two of these indeed were echoes which had travelled from the distant East, and so might, perchance, be allowed to die away unnoticed, but the third, circulating on the very frontier of Provence, could not be ignored, though it might, if the needful explanation were wisely accommodated to it, be converted from a rival into a useful auxiliary.

The first hypothesis was to the effect that Lazarus and his sisters, after the Ascension, continued in Judaea, there died and were buried. This idea is, according to the usual interpretation, implied or connoted in certain entries in Greek *Menaea* of the ninth and following centuries, and also in contemporary Latin *Martyrologia* (including even that of Ado of Vienne), in which the commemoration day of one or other of the three Saints is associated with Jerusalem, or with Bethania. And herewith fit in very well various stories which found some acceptance; such as that about the Bethanians having been among the witnesses present at the Dormition or the Assumption of the Virgin, either near Jerusalem or else in Ephesus, from which city they returned home; and another about the body of the Magdalene having been still in Jerusalem in the time of Charlemagne, who, in a celebrated Chanson de Geste,* of the eleventh century, which describes the journey of that Monarch and his twelve Peers to the Holy City, is said to have brought away, among other gifts received

---

* Charlemagne, an Anglo-Norman Poem, edited by Francisque Michel, London, 1836.

MEDIÆVAL LEGENDS

from the Patriarch, the head of Lazarus, along with the fostering arm of the aged Simeon, and a portion of the proto-martyr's blood. Such stories of course, by themselves, required no serious consideration, and as to the notices, above referred to, in Greek or Latin Martyrologies, scholarly partizans of the Provençal legend appear to have suggested in early times, as their successors have recently done, that in some cases Calendar entries, such as those referred to, designated localities with which the life, or some notable event in it, but not necessarily the death, of a saint was familiarly associated. It is recorded that the monks of St. Lazarus at Bethany, replying to interrogatories from Provence, disclaimed any tradition that Lazarus or his sisters passed their closing years within their town, and admitted that they had no special reason for questioning the Massilian story. And it may be here added that in numerous Itineraries, Chronicles, and other works, from the fourth century down to our own day, the mention of "Lazarus' tomb" or "Lazarus' house," or "the house of Lazarus and Martha" refers to the tomb and the house spoken of in the Gospel, and is not intended to indicate any locality for the later life, or the second death and sepulture of Lazarus.

The second hypothesis, without taking any specific notice of Martha, represented Cittium in Cyprus, and Ephesus, as the localities in which Lazarus and Mary Magdalene respectively passed their closing years, died and were interred. One of its two elements was disregarded by, and was perhaps unknown to, the author of the Life of Mary and Martha attributed to Rabanus Maurus,* but the other element was respectfully deferred to by him in constructing his narrative. For while he adopted and embellished the wildest fables about the mis-

---

* This Life is printed by Migne, ll. t. CXII., coll. 1431-1508, and by Faillon, *Monuments Inédits*, & C., ll. t. II., coll. 457-558.

sion of the sisters to Provence, he assigned, as his reason for excluding the brother from any share in that enterprise, that, according to the received tradition, he, having left his bishoprick in Bethania while persecution raged throughout the Holy Land, proceeded to Cyprus and exercised his episcopal functions there, surviving his restoration to life during 24 years.*

This tradition is not perhaps traceable to a very early period; for S. Epiphanius, though born at Eleutheropolis near Jerusalem, and though for many years bishop of Salamis in Cyprus, has told nothing about Lazarus, either in Judaea or in Cyprus, after his recall to life, but says only that, having been thirty years old at the time of that event, he lived for another period of thirty years.† It is however distinctly recognised, not only in *Menaea* of the tenth and subsequent centuries, but generally, by the Byzantine chroniclers who have had occasion to narrate the chief events of the reign of Leo VI., "the Philosopher." One of those events which occurred in Constantinople, and excited there a lively interest, was the erection by that Emperor, in A.D. 886 (or 890 or 901, for the dates vary) of a splendid church in honour of St. Lazarus, and the enshrinement within it of the body of the tutelar Saint.

Now while some of these authorities do not specify the quarter from which the honoured remains were transported,‡ others expressly state that it was from Cyprus, or more circum-

---

* Rabanus Maurus, ll. c. 35, ap. Migne, ll. t CXII., col. 1490.

† Epiph. Contra Haereseos, II., 66; cp. Faillon, t. I. coll., 361-3.

‡ See Symeon Magistros (or Metaphrastes), about A.D. 910, Chronographia, ed. Bekker, 1838, p. 704; An anonymous Continuator of Theophanes, commonly called Leontius, about 950, ibid. Lib. VI., pp. 364-5; G. Cedrenus, about 1050, ed. Bonn., 1839, vol. II., p. 260; Michael Glycas, after 1158, ed. J. Bekker, 1836, part IV., p. 554.

stantially, from Cittium.* But in regard to Mary Magdalene, the so-called Rabanus seems to have been unaware that not only Greek *Menologia*,† but also Latin authorities, to whom he might have deferred,—including Gregory of Tours in the sixth century, and the pilgrim-monk Willibald,‡ who described what he had witnessed at Ephesus in A.D. 745, had reported that her veritable sepulchre, not a mere cenotaph, was shown at Ephesus at the entrance of the Cave of the Seven Sleepers, a proximity which may have been accidental, or which may have implied that her body had been translated from some more obscure spot to the vicinity of the crypt, where the seven holy youths had slumbered from A.D. 250 to 479, and from which their mortal remains were subsequently removed to Marseilles. This localization is in harmony with a tradition, traced up to Modestus, bishop of Jerusalem in the seventh century,§ that Maria Magdalene, once a demoniac and a sinner, was martyred at Ephesus, having gone thither on a visit to St. John (who is believed by some to have been her betrothed), whether, as Modestus himself stated, after the death of the Virgin Mother, or, according to some variant accounts, while the Virgin was residing in that city with the Evangelist, her adopted son. A story found in some later authors to the effect that Mary Magdalene, not Veronica, was the woman who, after the Ascension, proceeded to Rome to expose the mal-

---

* See G. Monachus, a continuator of Theophanes of uncertain date, in Theoph. Continuatus, Bonn, 1838, p. 860; G. Codinus Curopalata, about 1453, De Aedificiis Const[is] ed. Bekker, 1843, p. 128.

† See *Kalendaria Ecclesiæ Universæ*, ed. Asseman, t. VI., p. 491; and also Nicephorus Callistos, *Sermo de Muria Magdalena*.

‡ Greg. Turon., *Gloria Murtyrum*, l. I., c. 30. Herzog, *Real Encyclopädie*, Maria Magd[a.], Band 9, S. 103.

§ See *Photius Bibliotheca*, Cod., 275.

THE HOLY GRAIL

versation of Pilate,* and induced Tiberius to recall him from Judaea, is not inconsistent with this legend, on the assumption that the Magdalene, having effected her object, returned to the East. This assumption is not only made, but insisted and dilated on, in the fullest and most curious account which we have of her journeyings, that given in a discourse by Nicephorus Callistos. This discourse states that she returned from Rome to a Phoenician port, and minutely traces her course through Palestine (where she abode for some time with the Virgin), Syria and Asia Minor, everywhere spreading the Gospel message, till she reached Ephesus, the place of her death and sepulture. And this is the more noteworthy, because the document which thus emphasizes her return to the East appeals, in regard to her success as an evangelist, to books of Italian authors (βίβλοις Ἰταλῶν); and further, it alone perhaps among Greek writings attests, cursorily but distinctly, that before she set out on her homeward voyage she traversed all Italy, and the adjacent parts even of the Gauls (διελθοῦσαν τὴν Ἰταλίαν πᾶσαν, καὶ τὰ πέριξ αὐτῶν Γαλίων); thus lending some countenance to the outskirt, though not to the body, of the Provençal legend.

It is further to be noticed that, according to the Byzantine Historians, the body of Mary Magdalene was transported by Leo VI. to Byzantium, and deposited in his new church there at the same time with that of Lazarus, and that two of them, G. Cedrenus, and G. Monachus, have mentioned

---

* See Constantinus Manasses, about 1150, *Synopsis Historica*, ed. Bekker 1837, vss. 1985-90, p. 86; Michael Glycas, *Annales*, ed. Bekker, part III., pp. 435-36; J. Cinnamus, *Epitome Rerum Gestarum*, VI., 8, p. 277 (ed. Aug. Meineke), Bonn, 1836. Cinnamus says that Mary chanced to touch at Ephesus on her voyage to Rome; Nicephori Callisti Hist. Eccles., II., X.

MEDIÆVAL LEGENDS

Ephesus as the place from which her body was translated.*
A third chronicler, G. Codinus (Curopalata), about 1453, has said that the two bodies were brought from Cyprus and from Bithynia; but, as he probably did not intend to differ from his predecessors, he may have made a slip, or at any rate written with laxity, in naming that province instead of Ionia. Or else, if "Bithynia" be a corrupt lection for Bethania, he may have by an oversight put down the name of the Judaean hamlet with which the family of Lazarus was associated, instead of the city from which the Magdalene's remains were directly conveyed to Byzantium.

Now, as to the relation which this legend concerning Cittium and Ephesus bears to that of Provence, while it does not fall within the scope of this work to examine it seriously, or to enquire which of the two has the less verisimilitude, we may here in passing notice the effect which a cognizance of the one legend had, or was likely to have, in modifying the views taken by the partizans of the other. That a writer like the so-called Rabanus,—whose credulity is incompatible with a capacity for drawing a strict line between fact and fable, and who evidently supposed the fictions which he was treating to lie within the province of history,—should have acknowledged and deferred to a Greek tradition regarding Lazarus, is really more surprising than is his disregard, or more probably his ignorance, of the parallel Greek tradition about the Magdalene. More consistent, though apparently less considerate were the writers, who, whether they had heard of discrepant legends or not, felt themselves bound as pious patriots to adhere steadfastly to that which promoted the honour of their country.

---

* Symeon Magistros; the so-called Leontius; M^l· Glycas; J. Zonaras; G. Cedrenus, as cited in note on page 114.

THE HOLY GRAIL

According to a third hypothesis, which for a long time was extensively prevalent, the remains of the Bethanian Saints were claimed by places within the Burgundian district, instead of Provence proper; or, to speak more definitely, since those districts overlapped each other, by Autun, Avallon, and Vezelay, all at tantalizing distances—so near yet so remote—from Avignon, Tarascon, Aix, and Marseilles. Of Martha indeed this hypothesis like the second takes no account, and so does not disturb either the reports about pilgrim visits to her tomb at Tarascon by Clovis, and many other distinguished persons,* or the allegation that, after a long concealment, it was again brought to light in 1187, ten years after which Invention a splendid church was there consecrated to her by Imbert, Archbishop of Arles.†

But the churches of Autun (the Roman city Augustodinum), and of its subordinate yet refractory neighbour Avallon,—each claiming to be the repository of Lazarus' remains,—and the church of St. Mary at Vezelay in the Diocese of Auxerre, as custodian of those of the Magdalene, were from the eleventh century downward, if not earlier, thronged and enriched by multitudes of pilgrims, including prelates and legates, nobles and kings, following out their pious vows, and, in later times, stimulated by indulgences. Among those devotees,—if the visits of some Carolingian Emperors be apocryphal,—we have authentic records of numerous Kings of the house of Capet, who thus from time to time recognised in Burgundy fit as-

---

* R. Maurus, ll. c. XLIX; also Vincent Bellovac, *Speculum Historiale*; cp. Faillon, ll. t. I., coll. 571-596.

† See Tillemont, *Memoirs pour servir à l'Histoire Eccles, des six premiers Siècles*, t. II., pp. 33-34;—and the abbreviated *Chronicon*, attributed to Hugo de S. Victor, which however closes A.D. 1190.

MEDIÆVAL LEGENDS

sociates for St. Denys, and St. Martin of Tours.*

The most conspicuous instances are Louis VII., who paid four visits between 1146 and 1171, the sainted Louis IX. in 1267, and Louis XI., who so late as 1469 was much perplexed between the rival claims of Autun and Avallon, in his anxiety to lay out to the best advantage the oblations by which the favour of *S. Ladre* might be secured. In course of time that strife came to be composed upon a mutual understanding that Autun possessed the Saint's skeleton,—only the skull, or part of it, having been gifted to the adjacent Avallon towards the close of the eleventh century, by Henry I. (le Grand), brother of Hugues Capet, and ancestor of what has been called the Second or Capetian line of the Dukes of Burgundy.†

How Autun and Vezelay came by their envied palladia was not explained in any definite or authoritative way. One bold assertion was that the body of Lazarus of Cittium (presumably therefore of Bethania) was brought from the East into Alsace in the eighth century; and another, to which we have previously referred, was that the remains of Mary Magdalene were brought from Jerusalem to Vezelay by its second abbat, Bodillon, shortly before or after A.D. 900. A more general credence was gradually attached to the view that, in one of the centuries during which the Mediterranean Littoral was ravaged by pagan corsairs,—first the Saracens, then Norsemen (Dani),—the expedient of secretly removing the remains of the most venerated saints to inland districts was resorted to, as likely to be more efficacious than the plan of merely concealing, or attempting to conceal, the sites of the original sepulchres. Thus the translation of the tutelars of Marseilles

---

* Tillemont, ll. Faillon, ll. t. I., coll. 819-867.

† Faillon, ll. t. I coll. 721-734; Devoucoux, Du Culte de S. Lazare à Autun, pp. 2, 8, 98 and 99.

THE HOLY GRAIL

and Aix to Autun and Vezelay was described as the pious work of ecclesiastics, acting under the direction of a Girard I.;—though as to who he was, and when he lived, the traditions were far from agreeing. In Autun he was generally identified with the Girard de la Roque, 46th bishop of that See, who is said to have effected the translation in A.D. 965, as attested by his successor in office Humbert, when he removed the relics from the old cathedral (*Eglise de S. Nazaire*) to the new one (*Eglise de S. Lazare*) in 1147. But it has also been supposed that the person intended was the same who secured the translation of the palladium of Aix to Vezelay, viz., Gerard, Comte de Roussilon, ancestor of what has been called the first line of the Dukes of Burgundy, to whom, with his wife Bertha, has been attributed the foundation of the Abbey at Vezelay.*

In the *Legenda Aurea*† the transference is ascribed to the first Abbat, Eudes, and a monk (by some identified with Bodillon, the second Abbat), in the interest of Girardus *Dux Burgundiae*, who is there said to have founded the abbey in the time of Charlemagne, viz. A.D. 769. The same date for Girard is given by various Trouvères writing in the Langue d'Oil, exemplifying a tendency, which has been observed both in the Carolingian and in other Cycles of Romance, to bring the personages of whom they treat into close proximity to the grandest figure of the central narrative, as his subordinates, or allies, or antagonists.‡ Various romances of the older class, and

---

* Tillemont, ll., t. II., pp. 32-4; Faillon, ll. t. I., coll. 721-34, 833-9; Devoucoux, *Du Culte de S. Lazare*, pp. 8-13, 32, 65-7, 75-7, 81, 95, 102, 115-17-18; *Maxine de Montrond, Dictionnaire des Abbayes et des Monastères*, Paris, 1856, col. 808.

† Legenda Aurea ed. Grässe, C. XCVI., p. 415.

‡ *So la Chanson de Roland*, Strophes 65, 164, 179, vss. 797, 2189, 2409, ed. Leon Gautier, Tours, 1876. Some rank this Girard, and

MEDIÆVAL LEGENDS

some chronicles in prose, represent Girard as a contemporary of Charles Martel, A.D. 715 to 741, affording an instance of the confusion between grandfather and grandson which has been often noted as characterising these semimythic narratives.* But we are informed in some later romances, referred to the 15th century, that Girard was a subject of *Charles le Chauve*; and this is the view which has been definitely established by historic investigation.† It is now clear that that Comte (or Duc) de Roussilon (not the city Roussilon (Ruscino) north of the Pyrenees, but a strong fortress near Chatillon-sur-Seine, on the borders of Champagne and Bourgogne), was appointed Regent of Provence by Lothaire, during the minority of Charles his third son, that between A.D. 850 and 860 he cleared the kingdom of his ward of its Saracenic and Norman invaders, who among their other outrages had sacked Marseilles, and that he returned to Bourgogne under Louis II., about A.D. 869, when, as has been conjectured, he took with him

---

his brother Doon of Mayence among the four sons of Aymon. So Renaud de Montaubon, p. 5, vss. 12-16, p. 13, vss. 28-35; Gaufroi, vss. 115-119.

* So la *Geste des Lorrains, Berthe anx grans Piés,* the Provençal *Girartz de Rossilio,* and the *Chronicle of Sigebert de Gembloux, Philippe Mousques,* and *Guillaume de Naugis.* The name Charles Martel is transferred to Charles le Chauve in the French *Roman de Girartz de Roussilon,* the *Reali di Francia* (v.c.9), and some other documents.

† See *Histoire Littéraire de la France,* t. XXII., pp. 167, and fol.; Paulin Paris, *les MSS. Français de la Bibliothèque du Roi,* t. III., pp. 114-5-6, and t. VI., 101-11; Raynouard, *Lexique Roman,* (where the Provençal poem is edited), t. I., pp. 174-5, 224, cp. p. 188; Fauriel, Histoire de la Poesie Provençale, III., pp. 34-8, 63-5; Gaston Paris, Histoire Poetique de Charlemagne, pp. 219, 220, 297-8-9, Ludlow, Popular Epics of the Middle ages, II., pp. 10, 11, 405.

THE HOLY GRAIL

the relics that were to enrich his newly founded monastery.*

Now the Burgundian claims, thus formulated, clearly recognised, and were themselves based upon, the antecedent rights of Provence; and Marseilles and Aix were alleged to have parted with their palladia only from a pious wish to save them from sacrilegious violation. Such deference to the Bethanian legend allayed the jealousy of its partizans. Accordingly the claims of Autun obtained a sullen acquiescence, though inarticulate demurrers were occasionally hazarded, and a vigorous protest was kept up that the skull, or at any rate the lower jaw bone, of *S. Ladre* had been always preserved in Marseilles, having been dexterously secreted, before the body was removed, by two good monks who contrived to substitute the head of some other saint. Accepting this compromise both cities might chuckle over the simplicity of the Avallonese, on whom the Capetian Duke Henri was now found to have conferred so cheap a gift.†

The pretensions of Vezelay however were more stubbornly, even if despondingly, resisted, and the relics of the Magdalene were averred to have been concealed only too securely from pagan marauders in some spot near Aix, or *La Sainte Beaume,* the traces of which spot had been lost from memory, but it was hoped might one day be recovered. The star of Vezelay culminated, between 1265 and 1281, within a church of which St. Magdalene had become the chief patroness about 1050; remains, certified as hers in an undated document, signed by a King Charles (whether *le Chauve* or *le Simple* is not clear), were brought to light in 1265, were visited by St. Louis and

---

* See besides Pn. Paris, Fauriel, and others quoted above, Faillon, ll. t. I., coll. 721-734, and Devoucoux, ll. pp. 101-2. coll. 12.

† Faillon, ll. 721-4; Devoucoux, ll. pp. 90-1-2, 98-9, coll. 59, 63, 68, 86, also the *Pieces Justificatives,* printed t. II., coll. 1291-1300.

the Cardinal-legate Simon,—who witnessed their elevation into a silver chasse in 1267,—and were commended to the faithful in Bulls of successive popes, the latest of which was issued by Simon himself, now become Martin IV., in 1281. But the Bull of Martin IV. was mistimed, too late, and ineffectual for its purpose. In 1269 Charles of Anjou, brother (or nephew) of St. Louis, who among his many titles had that of Count of Provence, and who ascribed his deliverance from an Arragonese prison to St. Magdalene, had the supreme satisfaction of finding the long forgotten, but still unrifled, sepulchre of his protectress at St. Maximin, and so vindicated the Provençal tradition against all doubt and rivalry, and secured the fame of *La Sainte Beaume* as a resort for pilgrims; just as the analogous Invention of St. Jago's bones in 816 had made the fortune of Compostella. Papal commendations were thereafter showered upon the hallowed site, which had been at last so marvellously revealed, while those previously lavished upon Vezelay ceased to be paraded, and the stream of devotion was more and more directed towards the south.*

Finally,—if the question were put whether the Provençal legend could be sustained, in competition with assertions that the relics of Lazarus, and of Mary Magdalene had been brought from the East into Alsace and Burgundy in the eighth and ninth centuries; the allegation that those relics had in the ninth century been still at Jerusalem; the tradition that they had been conveyed, towards the close of the ninth century, from Cittium and Ephesus to Constantinople, whence the Venetians boasted that they had brought away those of Lazarus, at least, to enrich his monastery in their own city;—

---

* See on Vezelay, Tillemont, ll. t. II. pp. 33, 34, 480, and Faillon, ll. t. I., pp. 833, 851, 863-7; and on St. Maximin, Faillon, ll. pp., 853-63, 867-77, 896-7, 916, &c.

THE HOLY GRAIL

what answer could be given by a Provençal patriot or hagiologist? What other than this,—that the claims of aliens might be espoused by rationalists, to whom treason appeared a venial offence if commended by historic criticism, but that he, for his part, must with his whole heart uphold the cause and the creed of his native land?

NOTES

Note 1, p. 8.

The texts of these documents published by J. Heroldus and J. Grynæus in *Orthodoxographa*, Bale, 1555, J. A. Fabricius in *Codex Apocryphus*, N. T. Hamburg, t. I., 1703, t. III., 1719, and A. Birch, *Auctarium* Cod. Apocr., N. T. Fabriciani, Havniæ, 1804, have given place to the fuller and more correct editions of J. C. Thilo, *Codex Apocryphus*, Lipsiæ 1832, and of C. Tischendorf, *Evangelia Apocrypha*, Lipsiæ, 1853 and 1876. The English Translation by W. Hone in the Apocryphal New Testament, London, 1820, based upon the old texts of Grynæus, is now superseded by that of B. H. Cowper, Apocryphal Gospels, London, 1874, which represents the recension of Tischendorf.

Note 2, p. 8.

The chronology of this composition, and its cognates, is most satisfactorily discussed by R. A. Lipsius, *Die Pilatus Acten*, Kiel, 1871. For the bibliography of the whole subject see R. P. Wülcker, *Das Evangelium Nicodemi u.s.w.* Paderborn, 1872; cp. A. Schönbach in *Zeitschrift für Deutsches Alterthum*, N. F. Band VIII. Heft 2, (1876), *Anzeiger*, pp, 149 and foll.

Note 3, p. 10.

On these vernacular versions and adaptations see Wülcker's work above referred to. His long promised re-edition of the West Saxon version, (published by Thwaites in his *Heptateuchus*, Oxoniæ, 1698), to be brought out by the Early English Text Society, will form a valuable accession to the materials already known.

Note 4, p. 14.

The designation Claudius usually points to the third emperor of the Gens Claudia, who reigned A.D. 41 to 54, and whose prenomen was the same as that of
the first of the imperial Claudii, viz. Tiberius. But the early writer, to whom this superscription is due, knew of course that each of the four immediate successors of Augustus was a Claudius Nero, and may have deemed it allowable to apply the name *Claudius* to Tiberius, the first of the four, or to the second, Gaius, usually known in Latin works by the pet name Caligula, which the soldiery bestowed on him in childhood. If the former interpretation be accepted, the anachronism at once disappears. If the latter be the true one, the writer seems to have assumed that the Procurator, in A.D. 34, addressed his letter to the same prince whom he found, on his arrival in A.D. 37, to have recently ascended the throne. And a reason for his addressing Gaius rather than his uncle is suggested in a statement appended to the Epistle in one of the Latin MSS., that Tiberius, though still reigning, was at that time laid aside by a grievous malady; see Thilo, ll. prolegg, p. 137. It would be more natural to attribute some share in administrative functions to the astute and aspiring prince, who was expected to succeed, and who did succeed his uncle, than to the shy and then generally contemned dullard, who did not come to the throne till A.D. 41.

Note 5, p. 14.

In the sense of "tradition" παράδοσις would be followed by περὶ Πιλάτου, as equivalent to "concerning Pilate," as παράδοσις Ματθαῖου denotes a tradition transmitted from Matthew, not one "concerning him." The usage of παράδοσις, as well as of the cognate verb, to denote a judicial handing over of a culprit for imprisonment or punishment is not unfamiliar both in Hellenic, and in Hellenistic phraseology.

Note 6, p. 16.

The mediaeval literature of the Legends of Pilate, and of the Destruction of Jerusalem, is most accurately, and all but exhaustively treated by A. Schönbach, *Zeitschrift für Deutsches Alterthum, N. F. Band VIII. Heft 2, Anzeiger,* pp. 167-212. He refers to Mone, *Anzeiger für Kunde der Deutschen Vorzeit,* 1835, 1838, also to Ed. du Méril, *Poésies Populaires Latines du Moyen Age.* Paris, 1847, pp, 340-368.

Note 7, p. 19.

In some versions of the story of Veronica, as we have noticed, she is introduced as the woman who was healed of the issue of blood (Mark v. 25-34), who in Greek text of the *Gesta Pilati* is named Βερνίκη or Βερονίκη, in the Latin Veronica.* In the Anglo-Saxon translation of the *Vindicta Salvatoris,* already referred to (page 17, note), there is a curious correction of the Legend. After stating that it was Veronica who touched the Saviour's garment and was healed, the writer adds, "She had a piece of the Saviour's garment and treasured it most dearly, and she accounted it even as Christ's own face," and as often as the *Dryhtnes Anawlyta* is spoken of this remark is repeated; "they (Tiberius, &c.) thought it was the Lord's face, but it was not so at all, but was the garment which the Lord Himself wore."

In *Le Roman du Saint-Graal,* where the story of Vespasian's cure is told at great length, Veronica tells that she met Christ on His way to Calvary, and gave a piece of linen (*Sydoine*)

---

* See Thilo, Codex Apocryphus, N. T., p. 560 and Note.

THE HOLY GRAIL

which she was carrying, to wipe the sweat from His face, and when it was returned to her she found His features imprinted on it.* In the different MSS. of the Graal she is called by various names, not "Veronica," which seems to be reserved for the portrait, but generally Veroïne or Verone; in the rhymed version of Robert de Boron "Verrine." These are only variations of spelling, but in some of the MSS., she has quite different names—*Marie La Venissienne, Marie l'Egyptienne, Marie de la Venience,* or *de la Venjence,* &c. The portrait is often named *La Veronique,* which is in favour of the conjecture of Mabillon that the name "Veronica" is formed from the words "*Vera icon,*" which were inscribed under the celebrated portrait of Jesus Christ preserved at Rome. Godwin, referring to this opinion of Mabillon (Anglo-Saxon Legends, &c. Introduction, pp. 7-8) adds "Certain it is that copies of this portrait were in mediaeval times distributed to pilgrims and visitants to Rome, under the name of Veronicae. In England they were called Vernicles, *i.e.,* Veroniculae." It is not quite clear whether he means the portrait we are concerned with, or the painting of Christ on cedar wood which is preserved in the chapel *Sancta Sanctorum* in the Lateran. In *Le Saint Graal* at all events, Veronica's relic is named *La Veronique,* and it is carried to Rome by Vespasian's messengers:—

> "Ainsi la semblance aportèrent;
> "On l'apele la Veronique,
> "C'on tient à Romme à grand relique."

Whatever may be the uncertainty about Veronica's name and personality, she has gained, and holds still, a place of

---

* See Le Roman du Saint Graal, publié par Fr. Michel, Bordeaux, 1841, pp. 65-8,74.

honour in the great Church of St. Peter in Rome, where her statue stands 16 feet in height under the Dome, opposite to that of S. Helena. In a niche above the statue is kept the *Sudarium*, the handkerchief which received the impression of the Saviour's face.* We find many notices of the estimation in which it has been held from century to century in Rome. Gregorovius, in his "History of the City of Rome in the Middle Ages," says "There is a small literature relating to the handkerchief (*Sindone*) of Veronica;" and he refers to a great many writers, Italian and German, who have given information about it at different periods. Roman tradition, he says, has continued the history of the *Sudarium*, and asserts that, after the cure of Tiberius, Veronica remained in Rome in possession of her treasure, till, dying at a hundred years of age, she bequeathed it to Bishop Clement, whose successors carefully guarded the relic till it was deposited by Boniface IV. in the Pantheon. John VII. at length removed it to the chapel he had erected in St. Peter's about A.D. 705, and there had it enclosed in a marble shrine.†

While Rome was under an Interdict, during the visit of Lewis the Bavarian, in 1328, when the greater number of priests had left the city and many of the churches were closed, the Handkerchief of Veronica, with other sacred relics, was carefully hidden; but in the year of Jubilee, 1350, though the city was in a state of desolation, churches and public buildings falling into ruin, "one solace remained to the pilgrims, that all the places which had been hallowed by legend, and

---

* Murray's Guide to Rome, p. 243, col. 2.

† F. Gregorovius, History of the City of Rome in the Middle Ages. Translated by Mrs. A. Hamilton, London, 1844. Vol. II., Book III. c. VII., pp. 195-8; Vol. VI., Part I., pp. 323-4; Vol. VIII., Part II., pp. 582-3.

all the relics honoured in the West, still survived. Of these none was more celebrated than the Handkerchief of Veronica. Chroniclers are silent concerning the likeness of the Saviour in the Lateran, formerly world-renowned, while they record that the Handkerchief (*il Santo Sudario*) was shown in St. Peter's every Sunday and festival day, and that the throng was so great that people were sometimes suffocated at the exhibition." In the fifteenth century the *Sudarium* was kept in an iron chest in S. Spirito, keys of which were possessed by six noble families. When the relics were exposed they were guarded by twenty armed men.

In the sack of Rome, May, 1527, when the city was taken by the army of the Emperor Charles V., the churches were robbed of their most sacred relics. "Everything was stolen, destroyed or profaned. A German soldier affixed to the shaft of his own spear the so-called sacred lance head; the Handkerchief of Veronica passed through a thousand hands, and through all the taverns of Rome. The great Cross of Constantine, from St. Peter's, was dragged through the Borgo and lost. Even the most sacred of chapels, the *Sancta Sanctorum*, was sacked." Most of the relics, however, were bought back from the plunderers, or in some way replaced, for they are still to be seen in St. Peter's, and in other churches where they had been enshrined. Veronica's Handkerchief, the Lance, and a portion of the True Cross, are still exhibited at St. Peter's at Easter, and on four other occasions during the year.

In the Cathedral of Milan, enshrined in a magnificent chapel, there is another relic bearing the same name *Santa Sindone*, or *Sudario*. It is venerated as a fold of the shroud in which the body of our Lord was wrapped by Joseph of Arimathea. Other folds, as is believed, of the shroud are treasured at Turin, at Lucca, at Besançon, and at several other places in Italy and France.

MEDIÆVAL LEGENDS

There is a very interesting ancient tradition connected with the *Hæmorrhousa*, which is quite distinct from the legend of Veronica that we have been concerned with. Eusebius tells (H. E. vii. 18) that, when he was at Paneas, a tradition prevailed there that the woman who was healed by Christ of an issue of blood (Mark v. 25-34) belonged to that place. Her house was still pointed out in the town, and there was there a remarkable memorial of the grace she had obtained from the Saviour. Before the door of the house there was a brazen statue, representing a woman kneeling at the feet of the erect figure of a man, whose hand was extended to her, while her hands were stretched out to him in the manner of a suppliant. Eusebius had seen this statue, as he says, with his own eyes, and he remarks that it is not to be wondered at that one who had been lately a pagan, and had received a benefit from the Saviour, should show gratitude in this way. He adds that he had also seen pictures of Christ, of Paul, and of Peter, and he finds in them an explicable imitation of the piety of the heathen. Victor Schultze, in his History of early Christian art,* quotes this passage of Eusebius, and—while he says that in the first centuries of Christianity before the time of Constantine, there were no portrait-statues of Christ, and that no statuary was to be seen in places devoted to worship,—that branch of art being discouraged or forbidden by the Church from the fear of its leading to idolatry,—he speaks of this statue at Paneas as an exceptional one, and finds reason to believe that it was really what tradition represented it. Other explanations of the figures were that they represented an Emperor and a personified Province, or Æsculapius and a patient healed by him, but Schultze regards these suppositions as untenable,

---

* Victor Schultze, *Archæologie der Alt-Christlichen Kunst*, München, 1895, pp. 285-6.

and holds that the position, and the description of the statue as given by Eusebius, are much more in accordance with the local tradition. The statue was destroyed during the reign of Julian.

Note 8, p. 22.

The form "Vigenna," which is found in some MSS. of the *Mors Pilati*, and is, in a French version of the 13th century, corrupted into Ingemia (certainly not denoting Geneva), can alone have suggested this etymological vagary. (In this explanation we have been anticipated by M. Ed. du Méril, ll., p. 367). It appears that a dangerous abyss or unfathomed pool in the Rhone, near Vienne, was called "The Hell Way" or "*Voie d'Enfer*" reminding us of "the hell of waters" in Childe Harold. See also Schönbach on this French version, ll., pp. 195-6 (w).

Note 9, p. 26.

These paraphrases and derivative works are fully catalogued by Schönbach, ll. pp. 167-170. The only work (known to the present writer) which does not appear in his list, being the old English Poem, Pilate, printed in Furnival's "Early English Poems and Lives of Saints," published for the Philological Society, Berlin, 1862, pp. 111-118. See also Du Mèril, ll. pp. 340-368.

Note 10, p. 34.

The poem of Robert de Boron of which we have given a brief outline, is generally acknowledged to be the oldest form in which the Legend of the Graal has come down to us. It is sometimes named *Le Petit St. Graal*, in distinction from *Le Grand St. Graal,* which also contains the history of Joseph and his family, with a great deal besides in its numerous episodes, which are drawn from a great variety of sources.*

There seems little doubt that the author of the *Grand St. Graal* was Walter Map, Archdeacon of Oxford, who was a man of great influence at the Court of Henry II. This work, and its continuations or successors, the Quest, Lancelot, Perceval, and other Romances which connected the Graal legend with the Knights of the Round Table, were written in England, while they inspired Chrestien de Troyes in France, and Wolfram von Eschenbach and other poets in Germany.

Robert de Boron's short poem, which contains all that is essential to the legend, confining itself mainly to the spiritual or symbolical meaning of it, has attracted little attention in comparison with the romances of chivalrous adventure, to which it had really given the inspiring idea. Whether it is a translation from an older composition in Latin, or the work of R. de Boron himself (who certainly does not claim originality), it is not difficult to divine the sources which have contributed to the Legend, and supplied nearly everything that we find in it. Adolf Birch-Hirschfeld,† a German scholar who has studied very carefully all the different works, prose and verse, which have embodied the legend, or into which it has entered, believes that Boron's presentation of it may have been wholly suggested to him by the earlier legends and traditions that he was acquainted with, in addition to what is told of Joseph, and of the events connected with the Passion, in the New Testament. We can see in his poem what a deep impression the account of the Last Supper especially,

---

* Le Saint Graal, publié par E. Hucher, Le Mans, 1875.

† *Die Sage vom Graal, ihre Entwicklung, &c., in Frankreich und Deutschland im 12 und 13 Jahrhundert, von Adolf Birch-Hirschfeld,* Leipzig, 1877.

THE HOLY GRAIL

and the fate of the false disciple (Matthew xxvi., 20-25) had made upon the writer. The legend owes much of course to the apocryphal gospel of Nicodemus,—to its second part, the *Descensus ad Inferos* which supplies the opening passage of the poem, and to chapter xv. of the first part, which describes the visit of the risen Saviour to Joseph in his imprisonment. Hirschfeld remarks that the Sacred Vessel is the only thing that remains to be accounted for as original in this legend. The absence of it would indeed be a fatal blank, but the mention of "the dish" at the keeping of the Passover, and its use at that solemn farewell feast, may well have supplied the idea of the Graal, and suggested the introduction of the consecrated Vessel as a symbol of that hallowed ordinance which was to be observed through all ages in memory of the Redeemer's death; and it would also suggest the separation between the true disciples and the false which took place at the first Service of the Graal. (Roman du Saint Graal, vv. 2555-86.) It is much more likely, however, that the legend existed in an older Latin version which Boron had become acquainted with, than that it originated with him.

Note 11, p. 36.

After M. Paulin Paris had published his account of the Arthur Romances, he met with a statement which quite changed his opinion as to the early connection of the Graal legend with Britain.* He had believed that, at a very early date, British Christians looked upon Joseph of Arimathaea as the founder of their church, and he was inclined to accept the theory that the "*Liber Gradalis*"† was really written by

---

* De l'Origine et du Developpement des Romans de la Table Ronde. Le Saint Graal, par Paulin Paris, 1872, pp. 3-4, 10, 17, 21, 28.

† Les Romans de la Table Ronde, par Paulin Paris, Paris, 1868,

MEDIÆVAL LEGENDS

some Welsh Clerk about the time, A.D. 717, that is assigned to the vision of the Hermit in the prologue of the Great St. Graal. But he afterwards found in the Chronicle of Senones, written by Richer, a monk of that abbey, that, in the time of Charlemagne, Fortunatus Patriarch of Grado (whom the chronicler styles Patriarch of Jerusalem) had brought among other sacred relics from the East "the body of St. Joseph, the decurion, the burier of our Lord," and had deposited it in the Abbey of Moienmoutier. There he remained, being elected Abbot, and the relics became the property of that abbey; but some time after,—the canons of Moienmoutier having become too careless in guarding their sacred treasures,—the body of Joseph was carried off by night by some foreign monks. Richer wrote his Chronicle in the beginning of the thirteenth century, and an Annalist of Moienmoutier somewhat later, quoting a list of the relics possessed by the abbey in 980, adds "*Exceptis corpore scilicet Josephi Sepultoris Domini, et aliis, per incunam clericorum alienatis.*" Thus we have evidence that, in the thirteenth century, it was not forgotten in the Vosges that the body of Joseph had been long possessed by the abbey of Moienmoutier, that it had been brought from the East, and that it had been carried away by some foreign monks. M. Paris thinks there is no doubt that these monks were from Glastonbury, and that the acquisition of this relic of Joseph may have been the origin of the story of his arrival at Ynys Wydrin in the first century, and may also have suggested the later story of his coming to Britain, with his son Josephe and his numerous followers, which is contained in Walter Map's version of the Graal Legend.

In Robert de Boron's version Joseph remains in the East, and waits for death "in the land where he was born," so that it

---

Tome 1, pp. 93-4, 102-5.

does not disagree with the tradition preserved in the Vosges. It was in that neighbourhood, while living in the service of Gautier de Montbèlial, that he composed his poem, as he himself tells us:—

"Je la retrais
"O mon Seigneur Gautier, en pais,
"Qui deMontbelyal estoit."

The Abbey of Moienmoutier was not far from Montbéliart, and it seems most likely that a legend of Joseph would be preserved there from the time that the Abbey possessed his body, and that it would come to the knowledge of Boron. He must have written before 1199, as in that year his patron Gautier set out for the Holy Land, and never returned to France. He died in Cyprus about 1212, and if M. Paris is right as to the meaning of "*en pais,*" the words quoted above must have been added to the poem after his death. But, probably before 1199 also, the great book of Walter Map had been written, which R. de Boron had heard of while he was composing his poem:—

"Le grant livre,
"Oû les estoires sunt escrites,
"Par les granz clers feites et dites;"

and Chrestien de Troyes had commenced his *Perceval le Gallois*.

So many of the Graal Romances must have been written nearly at the same time, in the last years of the twelfth century, or the first years of the thirteenth, that it seems as if they had sprung up at once by a common impulse, from some common source, which all the diligent search of later times has been unable to discover. Some of the writers refer vaguely

MEDIÆVAL LEGENDS

to a Latin record, said to be deposited either at Glastonbury or at Salisbury, but, if existing, it remained hidden, and no distinct account of it has been found.

There is some ambiguity about the meaning of the word "Graal," or Sangreal, as it is used in the Graal Romances, as to whether it was originally the name of the Sacred Vessel, or of the Book in which the Legend was contained. Though *grasal* or *greal* was a common term for a bowl or dish in several of the Neo-Latin languages, it seems to have become obsolete in Northern French, and the word is seldom used for the Vessel in any of the Romances. When it is first used in R. de Boron's poem it is explained as meaning "agreeable," because the vessel was *pleasing* to every one who saw it:

"Car nus le Graal ne verra,
"Ce croi je, qu'il ne li agrée."

It comes, of course, from the Latin word *gradale*, which in Low-Latin had two meanings. It was used for a *bowl* or *dish;* but *gradale* or *graduale* was also the name of the Service-book, or book of chants to be sung by the Choir in the Church service. We find the word "Graal" used in both senses, but M. Paris, in his painstaking study of it, was convinced that the latter was the sense in which it was first connected with the Legend.*

Note 12, p. 37.

On the association of Philip with John, or with

---

* See his note "Sur le Mot Graal," Romans de la Table Ronde, T. I. Addenda, pp. 378-80 ; also Rev. W. W. Skeat "On the Word Graal," in Joseph of Arimathie, &c. Early English Text Society, London, 1871. Preface, pp. 36-39.

Bartholomew, or with both, in Asia Minor, see Nicephoros, *Hist Eccles,* II., 39; *Acta Philippi,* Anastasius Sinaita, Symeon Metaphrastes, and various *Menæa* and *Synaxaria* referred to by Fabricius, *Cod. Apocr. N. T.* Pars II., pp. 738, 740-1, and exhibited by Tischendorf, *Acta Apostt. Apocr., Prolegg.,* pp. 31-37, and *Textus,* pp. 75-94, and *Apocalypses Apocryphæ,* pp. 145, 153-4. The whole subject of the Partition is fully discussed in Smith's Dictionary of Christian Biography, Vol. 1., pp 20, 21, 22.

Note 13, p. 40.

The Invention and translations of the remains of St. Stephen, and the miracles wrought by them, set forth by most of the Ecclesiastical writers of the fifth century, have been frequently described and commented upon by modern authors, including Tillemont, Fleury, Cave, Jortin, Gibbon, Alban Butler. See also Colin de Plancy, *Dictionnaire Critique.* Paris, 1870, t. I. pp. 284-9, coll. t. II., p. 211. and Dean Stanley in Smith's Dictionary of the Bible, vol. III., pp. 137-9.

Note 14, p. 50.

Having been tempted to offer one surmise, one may venture upon a second, in the comparative privacy of a footnote. The landing place of St. James while living, and that to which his mortal remains were transported long afterwards, is, by most writers, not vaguely located, but definitely placed in Gallæcia, the modern Gallicia; and it was a part of the same Gallæcia on the Atlantic Ocean to which, in the Pilate legend, Nathan, the bearer of despatches from Palestine to Rome, was wafted like another Odusseus by the winds and waves, and where he found Vespasian, or Titus, or both, exercising military authority. Now if any degree of improbability, greater or less, were to be considered in the treatment of legends, one might be inclined to ask whether "Gallæcia," in the Western stories, had not originated in a misconception of some Greek accounts, in which the destination assigned to both the messenger and the Apostle was Galatia (often spelt Gallæcia),— but not of course the Phrygian one but the Western or Gallia. At any rate upholders of the Apostolicity of Compostella, who have treated the ambiguity of the Greek name Galatia as a good missile wherewith to assail the claim of Gaul to be connected with Philip, might well have remembered the caution addressed to the inmates of glasshouses.

Note 15, p. 106.

It is stated by Simeon Metaphrastes, who is followed in our Acta Sanctorum, that the St. George, who is patron of England, Genoa and Venice, born in Cappadocia (like his Arian namesake the Archbishop of Alexandria), was religiously brought up, became a soldier and rose to high rank under Diocletian, but was martyred, after suffering torture, at Nicomedia or Lydda, April 23, A.D. 303, as his namesake, the Archbishop was, in Alexandria, in A.D. 361. His feast day is observed by both Greek and Latin Churches, the former calling him μεγαλόμαρτυρ and τροπαιοΦόρος. The latter has recognised it, at least since the time of Gelasius, A.D. 494.

Richard I. found his cult, as patron of soldiers, very popular in Palestine, and adopted him as his own Tutelar after the succour which he was accredited with giving at the siege of Antioch. The national celebration of his feast was enjoined by a council held at Oxford in 1222. Edward III. constituted him especial patron of the Order of the Garter, when it was founded in 1344 or 1350. It is, however, not easy to distinguish the details of his history from those of the Arian Bishop.

www.ingramcontent.com/pod-product-compliance
Lightning Source LLC
Chambersburg PA
CBHW071509040426
42444CB00008B/1569